COMPLEMENTARY HEALTH

OVERCOMING
STRESS

THE AUTHOR

Patsy Westcott is a well-known health and consumer journalist in the UK. She has had articles published in most national newspapers and women's magazines and has written thirteen books on health, childcare, and popular psychology. These include the best-selling *Alternative Health Care for Women*, which has been published in six different countries. She has two grown-up daughters.

The Institute for Complementary Medicine

The Institute for Complementary Medicine (ICM) was founded in Britain in 1982. It is a charitable organization whose aim is to encourage the development of all forms of complementary medicine, including research, education, and standards of clinical practice, and to provide factual information to the Media and the public. With over 370 affiliated organizations, the ICM sees complementary medicine as a separate and independent source of health care, yet it always encourages a correct relationship with the medical profession to ensure each case receives the most appropriate treatment available.

COMPLEMENTARY HEALTH

OVERCOMING
STRESS

PATSY WESTCOTT

SMITHMARK

A Salamander Book

© Salamander Books Ltd., 1997.
129–137 York Way,
London N7 9LG,
United Kingdom.

This edition published in 1997 by SMITHMARK Publishers,
a division of U.S. Media Holdings, Inc.,
16 East 32nd Street,
New York, NY 10016.

9 8 7 6 5 4 3 2 1

SMITHMARK books are available for bulk purchase for sales promotion and premium use. For details write or call the manager of special sales,
SMITHMARK Publishers,
16 East 32nd Street,
New York,
NY 10016; (212) 532–6600

ISBN 0–7651–9958–0

This book was created by SP Creative Design for Salamander Books Ltd.
Editor: Heather Thomas
Designer: Al Rockall
Production: Rolando Ugolini
Illustration reproduction: Emirates Printing Press, Dubai
Printed in Spain

Photography:
Studio photography by Bruce Head
The Image Bank: pages 12, 90, 93, 103, 106
Rolando Ugolini: pages 36, 37, 39

IMPORTANT

The information, recipes and remedies contained in this book are generally applicable and appropriate in most cases, but are not tailored to specific circumstances or individuals. The authors and publishers cannot be held responsible for any problems arising from the mistaken identity of any plants or remedies, or the inappropriate use of any remedy or recipe. Do not undertake any form of self diagnosis or treatment for serious complaints without first seeking professional advice. Always seek professional medical advice if symptoms persist.

CONTENTS

1

ASSESSING THE STRESS IN YOUR LIFE

Stress can affect any of us at any time. It can be caused by a whole host of life events—giving birth, getting married, or bereavement. And with life today moving at a faster pace than ever before, new stress factors, such as VDUs, mobile phones, jet lag and other aspects of twentieth century life, have been added to the stresses that humans have dealt with from time immemorial.

It's hardly surprising that according to a survey carried out in 1996 by the UK's Office of National Statistics, 60 percent of women and more than half of men claimed to have experienced moderate to severe stress over the previous year. Those in their mid thirties and early forties were most vulnerable to stress sparked off by work, relationships, and family pressure.

Being under excessive stress plays havoc with life: you feel exhausted yet you can't seem to sleep, your mind is whirring with the 101 things you feel you should have accomplished, you feel unable to concentrate on work or enjoy your spare time. Learning to deal with stress is very important, and not just because of these short-term effects. There is mounting evidence of the part played by stress in ill-health. The links between heart disease and stress have been well-established for a

number of years. However, a study in the *British Medical Journal* reported that breast cancer—suffered by one in twelve women in the UK—was linked to stressful events, such as bereavement, unemployment, divorce, and moving house.

Yet a life devoid of stress can leave you feeling bored and under-stimulated, and leading too quiet a life can be equally damaging to health. Research has shown that people living in the country, for example, are more prone to depression and suicide than those living in towns. As Hans Selye, the US psychologist who coined the word stress said, "Complete freedom from stress is death because all human activity involves stress." Quite simply, we need a certain amount of stress to make us feel alive.

Achieving a balance between negative and positive stress is a major challenge for the 1990s. This book offers you an active, practical plan for dealing with stress and transforming it into a positive force. In the chapters that follow you will learn how to assess the stress in your life, what warning signs to look out for, and what events and situations are most likely to cause stress. Using this information you can start to change your reaction to stressful events so they become more manageable, and thereby you can start to achieve a more balanced

Above: yoga is an effective way to manage stress in your life.

lifestyle. On a practical level, you will discover how eating a healthy diet, exercising regularly, and learning how to relax can help you combat stress.

Finally, you will get the chance to put it all together with a personalized stress management strategy. There is no one way of dealing with stress that is right for everyone. Throughout the book you will find, questionnaires and checklists which are designed to help you find the best way of dealing with stress and making it work for you.

WHAT CAUSES STRESS

Stress happens when we perceive the pressures of life to be too much to cope with and, as a result, experience mental and physical changes that threaten our well-being. No one escapes stress entirely. However, all sorts of factors, including the way you look at life, the amount of support you have from those around you, your living situation, the views and attitudes of people you live or work with, even the food you eat, can influence your susceptibility to stress and affect your response to it.

The degree of stress that we feel is determined not just by the things that happen to us but in the way we react to

them. Not everyone experiences symptoms of stress or goes down with a stress-related illness. What seems to be the deciding factor is not just the number or seriousness of stressful events that happen to us but the way we respond to them. For example, whereas one person might greet the prospect of organizing their wedding as invigorating, another might crumble under what they perceive as the overwhelming demands on their time and energy.

Below: telephones, fax machines, computers, and other facets of modern office life can all add up to extra stress at work.

STRESS TOLERANCE LEVELS

The secret of dealing with stress is to harness it so that it becomes a positive, creative force rather than something that drags you down. One way to do this is to train yourself to view stressors (things you find stressful) as challenges you are able to rise to meet rather than burdens which weigh upon you. A first step is to identify the things you find stressful and become aware of how you deal with them. Once you have learnt to recognize these factors you can begin to look at ways to prevent stress levels from building up and becoming harmful.

Most people find that their tolerance level varies at different times. Your state of health, your state of mind, even the weather, can all affect your reaction to stressful events.

For example, you may find that you are more able to deal with everyday nuisances of city life, such as late trains, crowded buses, noise, and pollution, in the summer when the sun is shining than in the depths of winter when everything else looks gray. If you are a woman you may find you are able to cope better with deadlines in the week after your period when you are feeling generally more calm and cheerful than in the week before it when you may be irritable and tense.

Most people also find that they can tolerate higher levels of stress in some areas of their lives than in others. For example, you may thrive on the challenge

Above: you can suffer from stress at home as well as at work. The birth of a baby can make your life more stressful, affecting your everyday routine, your sleep pattern, and relationships.

of pitting yourself against someone else on the tennis court but find it stressful if you are competing with someone in your office for a promotion.

Becoming aware of the factors that affect your response to stress will help you to monitor your stress level and if you find that it is getting out of hand, you should take steps to reduce it to a tolerable level again. Doing so will increase your feeling of being positively in control of your life and will boost your mental and physical well-being.

STRESSFUL TIMES

Sometimes the reason you feel stressed is an obvious event, such as getting divorced, moving house, losing your job, or being involved in an automobile accident. Such outside causes of stress are easy to pinpoint. However, at other times the sources of stress are less clear, because they come from factors inside yourself. Thus the feeling of strain when you feel overwhelmed by work may be partially caused by not organizing your time as effectively as you could. You may need to spend time examining how you are feeling to try and track the cause of your symptoms.

WORK STRESS

A survey carried out in 1990 by the UK's Henley Centre identified stress as a major concern in the workplace. Stress can arise from several different aspects of work. In the survey quoted, those on the highest rungs of the work ladder cited job stress as the most significant source of stress followed by traveling to and from work, and long hours.

The stress generated by the job itself is often linked to performance. Provided you remain confident and use up the energy and tension created by the extra demands on you, this can be a source of healthy stress bringing with it feelings of achievement and recognition. Those lower down found low wages, followed by traveling and job stress, most stressful.

Stress can also occur if you are working in an environment or a job that you consider is not really right for you. For example, you may feel that your abilities are being over- or under-stretched, that your position and career path are either too predictable or insecure. Alternatively, you may feel at odds with the goals and values of the firm you work for.

The immediate environment and actual working conditions can also be stressful. A noisy office or factory, working all day at a VDU screen, bad lighting, not enough space, the quality of the air, poor air conditioning, or inadequate central heating can all be sources of stress in your everyday life.

EVERYDAY ANNOYANCES

Managing stress is often easier when you are dealing with major identifiable

---

CHANGES IN YOUR LIFE

Many stressful situations are a result of change. Confusingly, sometimes the change is a happy or exciting event, such as getting married, having a baby, or falling in love. All these situations can cause an upheaval not just in your emotions but in the practical, everyday details of your life. Stress is often the result of feeling helpless and fearing that you won't be able to cope with the challenge of a new situation. Learning how to transform your feelings of helplessness by thinking positively can help you feel far less stressed.

problems rather than a mass of rather vague irritations. Some psychologists claim that it is not so much the major events in our lives that get us down as everyday hassles, such as forgetting where you have put your keys. When you are under a lot of stress you are less able to cope with situations that you would normally take in

Above: stressful events at work and in your everyday life can get on top of you, but you can learn to manage stress.

your stride. So stress leads to a lack of coping, which triggers off feelings of even greater stress and being less able to cope in an ever-dwindling spiral.

11

STRESS SCORES

Some psychologists have attempted to quantify the stressful impact of common events by coming up with a score for different experiences (see opposite). Not all these are unpleasant or undesirable but all involve change—for better or for worse. All changes involve feelings of both loss and gain and our reaction will depend on whether, on balance, we feel we have gained more than we have lost. For example, a move may mean leaving a house you love, losing touch with some of your friends, and having to give up a particular lifestyle which you enjoy. Or it could mean gaining in these areas.

This balance between loss and gain, the enormity of the change and the degree of control we feel over an event, together with factors such as our physical health and state of mind, will affect how we respond and how stressed we feel. To some extent, the major events in our lives—marrying, becoming a parent or retiring from work— are less likely to be stressful than the unforeseen stresses, e.g. being involved in an automobile accident, having an operation or a marriage breakdown. This is because we can plan for and anticipate them. For instance, research shows that retiring typically has little effect on mental health, whereas being unexpectedly made redundant or being demoted at work often takes a psychological toll.

THE STRESS CASCADE

Another factor to bear in mind is that one stressful event often sets in train other stressful experiences. Thus getting pregnant leads to the birth of a baby. Having a new baby who wakes several times a night leads to changes in your sleeping habits. Many couples find this disrupts their relationship; for example, they may row more often as they make the adjustment to parenthood. The new addition may also bring about a change in living conditions. Your home may suddenly seem too cramped, so you may decide to move and this involves taking out a large mortgage and getting a loan to buy new furniture—another source of stress.

Left: problems at work and long working hours can be a major cause of stress.

HOW IT ALL ADDS UP

Death of partner	100
Divorce or permanent split from partner	73
Personal injury/illness	53
Getting married/moving in with partner	50
Job loss	47
Getting pregnant	44
Having a baby	39
Change in financial position	38
Having more rows with partner	35
Taking out a large mortgage or loan	31
Being promoted at work	29
Child leaving home	29
Outstanding personal achievement	28
Change in living conditions	25
Doing more exercise	24
Moving house	20
Change in social activities	18
Change in sleeping habits	16
Going on a diet	15
Going on vacation	13
Christmas	12

STRESS LIMITS

All of us are more vulnerable to stress when several changes occur at once like this. There's a limit to the number of changes any one of us can cope with at a time. It makes sense if you can anticipate a major change to try to minimize the upheaval by avoiding other changes when you can. Many psychologists argue that to keep stress within manageable limits we should aim to have only one major change at a time. So, for example, if you have recently lost your partner through separation, divorce, or bereavement, it's best to postpone moving house until you have had the time to adjust to your changed situation.

You can see the scores for some common events on the stress chart (left). Have a look at it and then add up the number you have experienced in the last year. If you score more than 300 you are likely to be experiencing severe stress; if you score 200-300 you are likely to be feeling moderately stressed; and if you score 100-200 you may feel mildly stressed.

FINDING HIDDEN STRENGTHS

Some stress is unavoidable, of course, and this is not always a bad thing. The experience of navigating your way through a stressful experience can help you feel stronger and enable you to develop strengths that did not realize you possessed. It is rather like having a physical illness. The body mounts an attack on the invader by mobilizing its immune defenses, so that the next time you encounter the same threat the body fights back. The same can happen with psychological stresses. Discovering you have the resources to deal with a stressful experience or building them and knowing they can help you cope more successfully the next time you encounter a stressful situation is tremendously confidence inspiring and can mean you feel less stressed generally.

IDENTIFYING STRESS

Stress can manifest itself in several ways through our bodies, through our thoughts, through our feelings, and through our actions. But however you respond to stress, your reaction will be unique to you. For example, you may notice that the first sign that you are feeling stressed is you start to sweat, or you may notice your pulse rate soar. Alternatively, you may feel a warning ache in your shoulder blades.

Sometimes a minor illness is a warning that you need to pay attention to the amount of stress in your life. For example, you may always come down with a cold when you are under stress; you may develop a cold sore; if you are a woman you may suffer from thrush or cystitis. There are good reasons for this: research shows that negative emotions, such as stress and unhappiness, are communicated to our cells by means of chemical messengers. Stress hormones suppress immune activity.

Being aware of how you respond to stress by becoming aware of your body's personal warning signals can enable you to transform potentially harmful stress into healthy positive forms of stress before you are overwhelmed.

PHYSICAL SIGNS OF STRESS

Even when the stressor is something that affects us psychologically the first hint that stress is looming often comes not from the mind but the body. Our bodies respond to any sort of threat to their equilibrium by preparing us to either stand our ground and fight it or get away from it as fast as possible. This is known as the "fight or flight" response.

The fight or flight response is in fact a complex chain of physical and biochemical changes which are triggered by various stress hormones produced by the adrenal glands and released into the bloodstream to prepare the body for action. These are responsible for the typical symptoms of stress, such as a pounding heart, dry mouth, sweaty palms, and so on. These hormones also causes changes in the metabolism, releasing fats and sugars into the bloodstream to supply the body with the energy it needs.

THE EFFECTS OF AROUSAL

These effects need not be harmful if we do something active or have a period of relaxation after the stress has passed to allow the body to return to normal. However, if we are not physically active or if we don't consciously wind down, then the body remains in a state of arousal. For example, the heart becomes permanently over-worked leading to palpitations, fats may clog up the arteries, we may over-breathe, and the liver breaks down fats and protein and releases them into the bloodstream to provide energy which maintains high blood sugar levels. Eventually permanent changes may take

place in the body which can lead to physical conditions such as high blood pressure, diabetes, exhaustion, and a variety of other illnesses.

ADAPTING TO STRESS

When a particular stress goes on for any length of time the body may cease to respond to it. This is nature's way of protecting us from too much stress. For example, if you live on a busy main road you learn to screen out the traffic noise so

Above: family life is rewarding and stressful, especially when children are young.

you are genuinely surprised when someone visiting you comments on how noisy it is.

Each of us has our own individual tolerance level and while some of us easily adapt to sources of stress, others become even more aware of them. For example, if you have noisy neighbors you may cease to hear them playing their loud CDs after a while (unless it is in the middle of the night). On the other hand, you may become so aware of them that even the smallest sound from next door or the flat above makes you feel nervous. When this happens the body remains in fight or flight mode and the feelings of stress can become intolerable. Some psychologists argue that the inability to adapt to stress is what transforms otherwise fairly harmless occurrences into major sources of stress.

RECOGNIZING THE ALARM BELLS

Stress can trigger a whole range of both physical and emotional reactions. Many illnesses are recognized as being stress-linked. Even though they may not actually be caused by stress, stress may make them worse or prolong them. They include heart disease, high blood pressure, irritable bowel syndrome, premenstrual syndrome, rheumatoid arthritis, and skin complaints like acne and eczema. However, long before such illnesses strike there may be other warning signs that all is not well. Stress can trigger physical symptoms in any part of the body. At the same time, when you are stressed you may become more aware of odd aches and pains and may go to the doctor complaining of symptoms which you would barely notice if you were feeling less stressed. This can be a warning sign that you need to tackle your stress level. If you can learn to recognize the first twinges of tension in your shoulders, in the pit of your stomach, and the dryness in your mouth that signify that you are feeling stressed, you can take action to defuse them and reduce stress.

STRESS AND YOUR BODY

Eyes/ears/nose: the senses become more alert and send messages to the brain. The pupils of the eyes dilate to let in more light so we can see better.

Mouth: saliva dries up.

Brain: the brain sends signals to the rest of the body.

Muscles: the muscles tense in preparation to fight or fly from the danger.

Heart and circulation: the heart starts to beat faster. The blood vessels open wider so blood can circulate more freely. Blood pressure rises. Blood is diverted to the limbs in preparation for muscular effort.

Lungs: the air passages expand allowing more oxygen to be drawn into the lungs in preparation for fight or flight.

Abdomen: blood is diverted from the abdomen to the muscles slowing down digestion. Secretion of gastric acids increases.

Skin: sweating occurs, especially around the mouth, the temples, armpits, and hands and feet. The skin becomes pale as blood is diverted to the muscles. We are less sensitive to pain to protect us if there is physical injury.

Bowels and bladder: there's an urge to urinate and open the bowels to rid the body of excess weight should you need to flee the danger.

PHYSICAL SIGNS OF STRESS

- Breathlessness or sensations of choking
- Diarrhea and wanting to urinate
more often
- Exhaustion
- Feeling faint
- Headaches and migraine
- Indigestion and nausea
- Muscular aches and pains
- Palpitations and chest discomfort
- Spots and other skin eruptions
- Sleeplessness
- Tooth grinding or clenching the jaw
leading to headaches and facial pain
- Tremors and twitches

MONITORING YOUR THOUGHTS

When you are healthily stressed the mind reacts by becoming more sharply focused, enabling you to devise ways of dealing with the stress and overcoming it. However, if the stress continues for too long the mind gets tired and begins to suffer from overload. When this happens, you find it difficult to concentrate; making the smallest decision becomes a huge effort.

STRESS AND YOUR MOOD

One of the effects of stress can be to exaggerate your normal personality. If you are normally organized you become over-

Below: exercise and working out regularly can help to combat stress.

Above: it's easy to turn to artificial stress-relievers such as cigarettes and alcohol when you are under pressure, but they deplete the body of energy and make it harder to deal with stress.

meticulous; if you are usually anxious the slightest problem fills you with feelings of panic; if you tend to be easily aroused minor irritations send you into a seething rage; if you are an extravert you may talk too fast or too loudly; and if you are introspective you become anxiously preoccupied and locked in your thoughts. Some people become obsessive and they may focus on a particular thing such as their health, so they are always going to the doctor with minor ailments or taking medication for minor illnesses. Learning to recognize and deal with your own pattern of thoughts and feelings is an important part of stress management.

EFFECTS OF STRESS

Thoughts and feelings influence the way we behave and changes in behavior are an important sign of stress overload. Examples include becoming careless so you make trivial mistakes, driving more recklessly than usual, over-eating or under-eating, smoking or drinking more than usual, spending too much on clothes, or running up your credit card bill, working too hard or taking time off work, finding excuses not to do things, or going out all the time. You may notice a change in your sleeping habits. You may feel permanently tired and go to bed every evening at 9 o'clock. Alternatively you may find it difficult to sleep when you go to bed.

Prolonged emotional stress and strain are tiring and can cause a weariness which can be mistaken for physical tiredness. But often the answer is not to rest more but to do some physical activity or exercise to raise your energy levels.

CHAPTER TWO

CONTROLLING STRESS

We can't avoid stress but we can learn to live with it, change our response to it, and develop effective ways of dealing with it. By doing so, stress can become challenging and exciting rather than something to be feared. As we saw in the last chapter, much stress comes about because of change. Learning to deal with change in a positive way is the secret of transforming unhealthy stress into healthy stress.

A key factor in adapting to change is the ability to be flexible. This does not mean simply accepting what happens to you, although sometimes this is an appropriate response, but it also means choosing how you react to situations rather than allowing yourself to be dominated by habit. This act of choice helps you to feel more in control—an important factor in combating stress.

THE CYCLE OF CHANGE

Psychologists have identified five key stages of change. Research shows that many people go through these stages several times before the change is permanent. Just knowing this can improve your odds of dealing with change as the belief and confidence that you can handle things that may happen helps you to feel less stressed.

■ **STAGE ONE**

You are unaware or "under aware" that you are under stress. However, you may have begun to hear a few warning bells and may start to think about an aspect of your life that you are finding stressful, such as your work, your relationship or your health.

■ **STAGE TWO**

At this stage awareness increases and you begin to focus on the source of stress. You may begin to read specialist books or seek information about it.

■ **STAGE THREE**

At this stage you begin to take small active steps toward change by changing your behavior in some way.

■ **STAGE FOUR**

You begin to take even bigger steps by making more major changes in your behavior.

■ **STAGE FIVE**

Finally you start to reap the benefits of your actions and see some positive benefits from the change.

FACING UP TO CHANGE

This means being aware of the stresses in your life and the lives of others who are close to you, so that you can plan for them where possible. Take some time every day to look at the main areas of your life— relationships, work, your children, your

health—and become aware of them. Often you will be able to anticipate those areas that may become stressful in advance. Remember that there is no one "right" way to react to change. Some people are excited by it, others find it unsettling. Accept the

Above: a new baby can change your life radically, but will bring rewards and joy as well as new stresses.

way you are and allow yourself the time and space you need to adjust.

FINDING THE SUPPORT YOU NEED

When you are facing changes in your life it is important to have plenty of support from those around you. To do this you need to talk about what you are experiencing. It's not a sign of weakness to admit that you are under pressure. Research shows the value of having someone to talk to. This can be a relative, a friend, a work colleague, a member of a self-help group, or a professional counselor or therapist.

This person should be someone with whom you can share your emotions and feelings freely and openly without worrying that you will be judged or criticized. Sometimes it can be more beneficial to talk to someone outside your family and circle of friends, since people close to you often know you too well to offer impartial advice. They may lack the professional expertise to stand aside and allow you to find your own solutions.

Below: sometimes it helps to talk to a friend or counselor about your problems.

You are likely to need varying types of support from different people. There is the nurturing support of the friend who makes you a cup of coffee and listens to you, helping you to focus on your problems and solve them. Then there is the friend or colleague who helps you feel positive and inspires you to think up creative solutions to your problems. Finally, there is the relaxing support of the person who just allows you to be yourself so that you can recharge your energies ready for the fray.

A GOOD THERAPIST

Whether it's a friend in whom you have confided, or a professional counselor, a good therapist should follow certain basic rules. It's your right to be believed, valued and supported, and to know that what you say is totally confidential.

1 A therapist should never start telling you about his or her own personal problems, or compare your problems with their own. Even situations that seem superficially similar on the surface are completely different.

2 Beware of any therapist who appears to be trying to put words into your mouth or planting recollections of traumatic events, such as sexual abuse, by asking leading questions. A therapist should give you time to tell your own story in your own way.

3 A therapist should never tell you directly what to do. The idea of therapy is to help you to find your own solutions.

4 Needless to say, a therapist should never try to touch you in a sexual way, ask you to undress or talk suggestively to you.

5 Beware of a counselor who believes in keeping a family together at all costs, despite problems such as physical or sexual abuse, or deteriorating health and mental well-being.

6 Beware of any therapist who doesn't believe you, suggests that your problems are all your own fault, blames you for abuse, or suggests that you "get something out of it."

7 Steer clear of any therapist who doesn't make you feel cared for, encouraged, and supported, or who actively humiliates or criticizes you.

8 If you still don't trust your therapist, or feel safe with him or her, even after several sessions, or if your therapist gossips about your confidences, then you should stop seeing him or her immediately.

9 If, even after working together for months, you see no change in yourself or feel you are not learning anything new, then the therapy is probably a waste of time.

10 Beware of any therapist who promises an instant fix—especially if the therapist has a hobby horse, such as a particular religion, or type of therapy such as hypnosis. Remember that most longstanding problems take some time to sort out.

11 Beware of any therapist who tries to extort large sums of money from you. Make sure that you discuss the cost of therapy and agree a scale of fees in advance of the sessions.

THINKING YOUR WAY OUT OF STRESS

A key quality for dealing with stress is the belief that you are in charge of your life. If you believe that outside forces and other people are responsible for the way your life goes you are more likely to feel numb, victimized, helpless, or angry in the face of change.

Often what we believe tends to happen. Experts call this a self-fulfiling prophecy. So if you believe what happens to you is out of your control then you will act in a way that confirms your beliefs. If, on the other hand, you believe you can do things to make your life better, then your actions

will confirm this. Learning to believe in yourself can help you manage both the big changes that happen to you and also the small, constant ones.

Each one of us has our own unique way of thinking which helps us to decide on the way we approach problems. Sometimes, however, negative messages from the past can dent your belief in your ability to meet problems successfully.

Below: the way you think about the world can determine how stressful you find events and situations that occur.

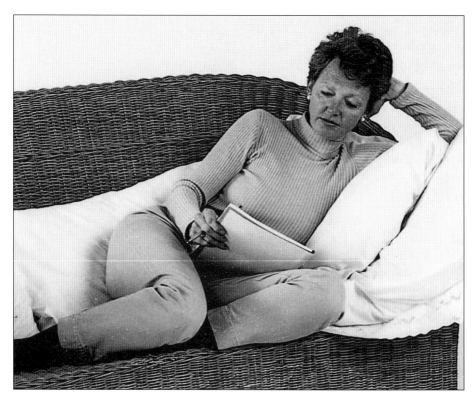

Having a healthy sense of self enhances your ability to deal with problems. It allows you to shrug off hurtful criticism, to appreciate compliments, and to have a realistic idea of both your strengths and weaknesses. If you lack self esteem, you may feel that you cannot rely on yourself and so avoid taking risks. As a result you suffer great stress if you have to deal with new or unfamiliar situations and approach problems beset with doubts and fear of failure—all of which can make a stressful situation worse. Examples of such negative thoughts include:

■ "Something is bound to go wrong."

■ "I'm sure to make a mistake."

■ "Nobody likes me really."

DEVELOPING YOUR SELF ESTEEM

Learning to see changes and crises as opportunities will help you gain the self-confidence you need to deal with stress. The key to developing strong self esteem is to separate the way you feel and think about yourself from the way that others feel about you. This may seem difficult, but it is just a matter of practice.

As a first step, make a list of all the things you like about yourself. Include any aspects of your physical appearance that you like, such as a friendly smile, social skills or aspects of your personality, warm manner, events, experiences, thoughts and feelings that you feel particularly pleased or proud of, and risks taken. Think of your skills and abilities; the things you have achieved or done well, big or small;

HOW POSITIVE ARE YOU?

Study the following statements and answer "yes" or "no" depending on whether they apply to you.

1 Success at work comes from being in the right place at the right time.

2 My income is more a matter of luck than ability.

3 I have little control over what happens to me.

4 Success depends more on luck than good planning and hard work.

5 I would be happier if it weren't for wars, famine, disease and all the other problems in the world.

Scoring: if you answered mainly "yes," you believe that what happens is out of your control and you are likely to find it harder to withstand stress. If you answered mainly "no," you believe you are in charge of your own life and what happens to you. This makes it easier for you to thrive when things go wrong.

standing up for your beliefs, appreciating your surroundings. Remind yourself of these regularly. In this way you can buffer yourself against insensitive comments from others, which will enable you to deflect criticism, and strengthen and sustain yourself psychologically. It also helps you to gain confidence so that you feel you can cope with whatever happens because you know you have inner strengths that you can bring to bear on any situation in which you find yourself.

BEATING THE BARRIERS

Sometimes negative thoughts, feelings and actions help to protect us in the face of stress or change. However, in the long-term they can stop us from dealing with problems effectively. The higher your self esteem the fewer of these defense mechanisms you will need to employ because you will have the inner certainty that you can deal with any challenges. Examples of unhelpful defenses include:

■ Feeling afraid to say what you think and thus staying silent.

■ Telling yourself that something which you think is important doesn't matter.

■ Going onto the attack before you can be hurt.

■ Standing your ground—even if your position becomes untenable.

■ Acting as though you are bored to disguise uneasiness.

■ Putting yourself down by telling yourself "I must be stupid."

■ Over-riding anyone who disagrees with you.

■ Switching off by retreating behind a newspaper, reading a novel, switching on the TV, playing with your computer.

■ Acting silly to distract yourself and others from the true problem.

Sometimes we fall back on these defenses when a situation that we find ourselves in conjures up an occasion when we felt we couldn't cope in the past. It could be triggered by something that someone says. Sometimes it's not the words themselves that you hear but how

Above: learning to think positively can enable you to deal with stress effectively.

they say it—the loudness, tone of voice, the speed. These can spark off a memory of a particular scene, a sudden feeling that you've been here before.

Learning to recognize how your defenses have served a useful purpose in the past, but that now they are limiting you, can be a way forward. Whenever you find yourself thinking, feeling or acting in an unhelpful way ask yourself the following questions:

■ What am I defending myself against?

■ Why do I need to defend myself?

■ Do I need to change my defense mechanisms?

Do this every time you find yourself reacting defensively and you will learn to let go of your defenses and behave flexibly.

BEATING THE NEGATIVES

Learning to think and act positively is an important part of dealing with stress both at home and at work. This can help you to identify unhelpful ways of feeling and thinking and offers some suggestions as to how to combat them.

 Feeling sorry for yourself?

 Don't allow yourself to wallow in self-pity and bear in mind that you are not alone. Send yourself some supportive messages such a "I'm not the only person ever to have this problem." You may like to talk to other people who have gone through the same experience, perhaps among your friends, relatives, or colleagues, or by contacting a support group.

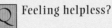 **Feeling overwhelmed?**

 Laugh it off. Learning to see the humor in stressful situations can help make the situation more tolerable. Build up a collection of amusing books, videos, stories, and so on that you can turn to when life is getting you down, or spend time with a friend who makes you laugh.

Feeling out of control?

Recognize that there is often a pattern to "unexpected" problems. When facing a problem think through how it happened and try to pinpoint the most likely causes. These can often point the way to possible solutions. Check any solutions you come up with to make sure they address the causes you have identified. If you get into the habit of doing this you will find it easier to solve your problems.

Feeling helpless?

Think of situations you have encountered in the past where you have overcome obstacles and found the courage to cope. These may be either similar or other difficult situations. Think about which skills you harnessed, and recall how you dealt with previous problems. Concentrate on the positive factors in how you coped rather than the negative ones.

Feeling trapped?

There always is an alternative course of action if you allow yourself to think creatively. This may involve scrapping your original plan and redrawing it. You may need to analyse why your present coping strategies are not working. List all the possible new solutions you can think of without censoring them. Give yourself time and don't make hasty decisions. If you don't try to force it your brain will often do the work for you.

LOOKING AFTER YOURSELF

When facing a period of stress in your life, you must look after yourself physically. Eating a healthy diet plays an important role in this.

A HEALTHY DIET

This is vital because if you are not properly nourished you may find yourself unable to think clearly and your feelings may be muddled. Eating properly helps you feel more energetic and vital so you are more able to tackle sources of stress.

Below: a healthy diet containing fresh fruit and vegetables will give your body the nutrients it needs to withstand stress.

■ **The secret of healthy eating**, as with many other aspects of successful stress management, lies in getting a balance that is right for you. We have different needs at different ages and stages of our lives. For example, the needs of a pregnant woman are different from those of a teenager, while people who are physically active need different nutrients to couch potatoes.

■ **Obesity and dieting** can also sap energy and add to stress. Research shows that women on diets make on average 20 percent more errors through tiredness than non-dieters. Dieters also find it harder to get the amount of nutrients they need because they don't consume enough food. And if that isn't enough to persuade you, dieting actually slows down the body's metabolic rate—the rate at which energy is burned—leaving you with fewer resources to fight stress.

THE COMPLEXITY OF CARBOHYDRATES

You should also step up your intake of complex carbohydrates. These include potatoes, sweet potatoes, and whole-grain cereals for slow release of energy. Whole-grain products are more nutritious than the white varieties, which have had virtually all their nutrients removed. However, go easy on the bread, especially the white sliced variety, as it contains too much wheat, yeast, and gluten. These are the main ingredients in bread and they can be difficult to digest and cause allergies which in turn cause fatigue. Alternatives to white

---

CHOOSING THE RIGHT FOODS

■ Fresh, preferably organic, food is the best for health.

■ You should cut down on processed, convenience foods and aim to eat at least five portions of fresh fruit and vegetables a day. Buy them fresh; keep them for as short a time as possible and keep cooking times to a minimum (stir-frying and steaming are good methods) to preserve the maximum amounts of nutrients in the food.

■ Try to ensure that some of the fruit and vegetables you eat are raw (some experts claim that 60 percent of the diet should be raw).

■ Fruit and vegetables are rich sources of the ACE vitamins— vitamins C, E, and beta carotene (converted in the body into vitamin A). These vitamins occur naturally in vegetables such as carrots, broccoli, tomatoes, citrus fruits, nuts, and whole-grain bread.

■ B group vitamins are also important when you are under stress as they help create a healthy nervous system. Another vital nutrient is Omega-3, a fatty acid found mainly in oily fish, e.g. tuna, salmon, and sardines, which helps maintain a healthy heart and blood vessels.

---

sliced include yeast-free soda breads, wholemeal pita, sourdough loaves, and whole-grain pasta. If wheat causes problems for you, try rye bread, cakes or crackers, and other starches, such as brown rice, couscous, quinoa, millet, and oats.

TAKE CARE WITH FATS

Polyunsaturated or monounsaturated fats are found in nuts, seeds, corn, avocados, olives, and oily fish and their oils. These oils are usually liquid at room temperature and are preferable to the unsaturated (generally hard) fats found in meat and dairy foods. They help promote a smooth circulation, healthy heart and blood vessels, and also are necessary for the brain to function well—essential when you are under stress.

■ Opt for white meats, such as chicken or game, which contain fewer harmful unsaturated fatty acids.

■ Step up your intake of oily fish, such as tuna, salmon, and swordfish.

■ Virgin or extra-virgin, cold-pressed olive oils are the best for health.

CUT OUT JUNK FOOD

As well as making sure that you eat the right foods you need to avoid the wrong ones. Certain foods and eating patterns drain energy and stress the body physically. Potato chips, corn snacks, and cookies, known as simple carbohydrates, are particularly damaging. They give you a quick fix by releasing glucose into the bloodstream. However, in the long-term they cause blood sugar levels to plummet. Too much sugar can also cause the overgrowth of the yeast candida, which is also implicated as a factor in chronic fatigue and tiredness.

NOURISHMENT MATTERS

■ Base your diet on starchy (carbohydrate) foods, e.g. potatoes, bananas, whole-grain cereals, and pasta, which help supply the muscles with instant energy.

■ B vitamins, which are found in whole-grain cereals, meat, fish, nuts, bananas, and pulses, and in particular B1 (found in whole-grain bread and cereals, pork, beans, and lentils), are needed if you increase your energy intake by eating more starchy food.

■ Folic acid, found in green leafy vegetables, oranges, and bread; B12, found in meat, fish, dairy foods, fortified cereals, and yeast extract; iron, found in meat and pulses; and vitamin C, found in many fruit and vegetables, are vital to form red blood cells which carry oxygen to the muscles.

■ Make sure you get a good daily supply of vitamin C to help combat winter colds and other infections. It also helps the body to absorb iron.

■ Eat oily fish three times a week or take a supplement containing Omega-3.

FOODS TO COMBAT STRESS

The following offer a good supply of the ACE vitamins (see page 29) and minerals: sweet potatoes, carrots, watercress, peas, broccoli, cauliflower, lemons, mangoes, meat, melons, bell peppers, pumpkin, beans, strawberries, tomatoes, cabbage, grapefruit, kiwi fruit, oranges, seeds and nuts, squash, tuna, salmon, wheatgerm, and apricots. Make sure that you include them in your diet.

MANAGING STRESS AT WORK

Most people spend eight hours a day (at least) working and that's not to mention the time spent traveling to and from the workplace, so it's not surprising that work-related stress is one of the biggest hazards to health.

Some jobs are obviously stressful because of the nature of the work involved—for example, air traffic controller, pilot, doctor, or police officer. However, in many cases stress arises because of specific aspects of the working environment. Stress factors on the job include: long hours and adverse working conditions, especially too much noise, constant interruptions, poor lighting, heating and ventilation, pay disputes, overwork, new technology which places extra physical and mental demands on employees, and shift work, which disrupts the body's daily rhythms.

Below: the nature of the work you do as well as particular aspects of your work environment can create stress.

Other pressures may come from feeling that you don't have a clear role at work, whether you feel your contribution to the job is recognized and appreciated, and from your relationship with your boss.

■ Learn to manage your time. Set yourself goals, and divide big jobs into smaller ones so you can feel a sense of achievement as each part of the task is completed.

■ Try to do the most unpleasant, boring jobs at times of low energy, e.g. after lunch when energy levels tend to be lower.

■ Take regular breaks. Our powers of concentration dwindle every 45 minutes. You will work more effectively if you take regular breaks. Stand up and walk around the office, make some coffee, or do a few simple stretches at regular intervals.

■ Say "no" to any interruptions. Put the telephone on an answering machine and do your phoning in a batch to avoid constant interruptions.

■ Focus on what you have to do. Clear your desk and put things away as you complete each job to avoid clutter and help you concentrate on the job in hand.

■ Personalize your work space with photos, plants, postcards, and so on.

■ If you are a boss, you should recognize that stress is part of the job and encourage an understanding and acceptance of it; try to improve communication at work and participation at all levels; always offer encouragement and constructive criticism.

EYE EXERCISE

Working for long periods at a VDU screen is very tiring for your eyes and can create eyestrain and headaches in office workers. To avoid eyestrain, you should not stare fixedly at the screen without taking frequent breaks, at least once every hour. If your eyes start to ache, try this simple exercise. Raise your hand about 18 inches away from your face. Point your forefinger and focus intently on it. Move your finger slowly from side to side, then up and down and round and round, following it with your eyes but without turning your head.

OFFICE STRETCHES

Sitting at your desk all day with few breaks can cause a variety of aches and pains, especially backache and headaches. If you tend to sit hunched up, you should take time off work every hour to do some simple stretches at your desk.

1 With one arm hanging over the arm of the chair, lean to one side. Feel the stretch in your neck and the side of your body.

2 With your hands resting on the arms of the chair, turn your head to either side, feeling the stiffness ease out of your neck.

3 Now lean forward, letting your arms and head hang down. Feel the stretch in your spine.

4 Tilt your head over to one side, then backward and forward. Rotate it gently. Breathe in deeply and resume working.

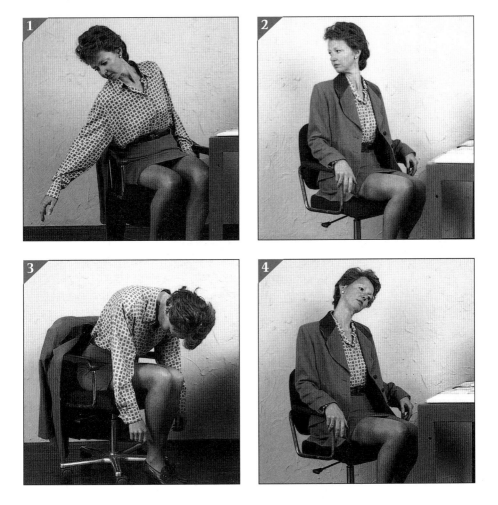

EXERCISE

E xercise is a positive way to prevent stress overload. During periods of stress the body gets ready for action. If no activity is then required, the muscles remain tense and tight, the stress hormones don't get discharged and we feel tired and our bodies ache. Exercise helps to reduce tension, prevents stress from accumulating, helps you feel more relaxed and sleep better. Being physically fit ensures that your body functions efficiently and is

better equipped to cope with extra stress.

Research shows, for example, that women who exercise regularly suffer fewer premenstrual syndrome (PMS) symptoms and are happier at all times of the month than those who are sedentary. At the same time exercising releases endorphins: feel-good hormones that help improve our confidence, boost self esteem, and lift our mood. They make us feel more energetic and positive about life.

FIRST FIND YOUR FITNESS LEVEL

Fitness is not just measured by how many step classes or games of tennis you do in a week but in how much activity you get in your everyday life. Use the following quiz to assess your overall level of fitness.

1 In a typical eight-hour day how much time do you spend being active and moving around (this includes walking to the stores, doing housework, walking up the stairs rather than taking the elevator, and so on)?

a Hardly any ☐
b Less than two hours ☐
c Between two and four hours ☐
d More than four hours ☐

2 How often do you lift or carry shopping, a child, or other objects weighing more than 14 pounds?

a Hardly ever ☐
b Up to five times a day ☐
c Six to 20 times a day ☐
d Over 20 times a day ☐

3 In a typical day is most of your time spent as follows?

a Sitting down ☐
b Doing some light activity, e.g. housework, looking after a young child, typing ☐
c Doing something physically strenuous ☐
d Doing something very strenuous physically, e.g. bricklaying ☐

4 In a typical working week how much time do you spend in light activity, e.g. walking or cycling to and from work?

a Less than one hour ☐
b One to two hours ☐
c Two to four hours ☐
d More than four hours ☐

5 In a typical week how much of your spare time do you spend in light activity, e.g. golf, light gardening, gentle swimming, walking in the country, doubles tennis, or badminton?

a Less than two hours ☐
b Two to three hours ☐
c Three to four hours ☐
d More than four hours ☐

6 In a typical week how much of your spare time do you spend in vigorous activity, e.g. having a game of rackets, running, step classes, hard swimming, singles tennis, disco or Latin dancing?

a Less than one hour ☐

b One to two hours ☐
c Three to four hours ☐
d More than four hours ☐

7 If you used to have a leisure interest which involved strenuous activity how long ago did you give it up?

a More than six months ago ☐
b Less than six months ago ☐

8 How often do you run up or down stairs?

a Hardly ever ☐
b Sometimes ☐
c Often ☐
d Always ☐

Scoring: score one point for each time you answered a; two for b; three for c; and four for d.

■ **8–15** Your life involves very little physical activity and there is plenty of room for improvement. Have a look at your lifestyle and work out ways in which you could incorporate more activity into your everyday life, e.g. by using the stairs instead of the elevator, or carrying shopping rather than doing it all by car. When you have made these small improvements try to make time for regular physical exercise. For example, enroll in an exercise or yoga class, go swimming regularly. Build up your activity levels gradually.

■ **16–24** You are moderately physically active and should have a reasonable level of fitness. It is vital to maintain this by continuing to be as active as you can in your everyday life. You would also benefit from undertaking a regular exercise program if you don't do so already. Aim to play a sport, do an exercise class, or do something physically strenuous at least three times a week.

■ **25–32** You are generally physically active and should have the physical stamina to cope with most of the challenges you are likely to encounter. You may want to increase your mental fitness by taking up an activity such as yoga. Don't try to do too much, have a rest occasionally, and pay particular attention to stretching, warming up and cooling down.

GETTING STARTED

Exercise does not have to be frenetic to be beneficial and there's a sport or exercise for you, no matter what your lifestyle. It's all a question of finding something that feels right and fits into your daily life. Forcing yourself to do gruelling aerobics sessions if they bore you breeds resentment—and stress. However, if you take the time to select an activity you enjoy you are more likely to stick to it.

■ Aerobic exercises, such as walking, swimming, or running, help take your mind

off your worries, exercise your heart and release endorphins which increase feelings of well-being.

A good way to get started is to join a gym or work out regularly. You can choose between weight training, running, cycling, and step-up machines, and you may make new friends, too.

■ Exercises such as yoga, T'ai chi, and Pilates involve mental as well as physical discipline and help you to distance yourself from problems so you can get them more in perspective.

Above: aerobic exercise, such as cycling, tones up the heart muscle and causes the body to produce endorphins, the body's own stress-relieving hormones.

FINDING THE ACTIVITY THAT IS RIGHT FOR YOU

The advantage of gyms and fitness classes is that the routines are specially designed and monitored by qualified instructors, whereas activities such as sports or dance may be more stressful because of risks which are outside your control, such as slippery floors, fast-flying balls, or any unexpected twists or movements. The best plan is to seek advice on proper exercises. Keep an eye out for new developments and make sure any books or videos you buy are presented by qualified instructors, rather than supermodels or celebrities.

Recognizing and then harnessing your motivation are also important. Some people are motivated by the challenge posed by a sport or exercise, others by their enjoyment of being outside in the fresh air, being part of a team or the opportunity to get to know new people. Looking at the sorts of exercises you have enjoyed in the past can help identify the sort of exercise that is likely to suit you now. You may like to take up specific sports or exercises you enjoyed in the past and build on your skills. Alternatively, you may notice that you have always opted for exercises that you do in a group, in which case sociability may be a motivating factor and you may do better joining a class or a club. However, if you've always gone for solitary activities, such as swimming, you may get on well with an exercise video or taking up something like windsurfing, which you can do alone.

If you get bored easily it will probably be best to try a sport or exercise which involves developing progressive levels of skill, such as tennis or contemporary dance, rather than aerobic exercise which tends to be repetitive.

MIX AND MATCH

Another way to beat boredom and avoid stressing your body is to cross-train; in other words, vary the exercise you do. This involves varying your fitness programme to include some cardiovascular exercise, some exercises for muscular strength and stamina, and some stretching.

Cross-training has another advantage: most injuries are a result of repetitive stress to the same part of the body so varying what you do gives your body a

CAUTION!

Before embarking on an exercise program, you should consult your doctor if you have any of the following conditions:

■ You have heart disease, high blood pressure, or any other cardiovascular problem.

■ A history of heart disease in your family.

■ You experience pains in your heart and chest on exertion.

■ You get headaches or feel faint or dizzy.

■ You suffer from pain or limited movement in your joints when you exercise.

■ You are taking some medication for a pre-existing medical condition or you are recovering from a recent illness or operation.

■ You are pregnant.

■ You are unaccustomed to exercise and aged over fifty.

■ You have a pre-existing medical condition which may affect your ability to exercise.

SELF-ASSESSMENT TEST

Your exercise history and how you think and feel about exercising can influence your motivation, attitude and the type of exercise you choose. The following self-assessment test is intended to get you thinking about what exercise would be best for you.

1 How much time do you have for exercising?

2 Do you prefer to exercise alone or in company?

3 Do you prefer to exercise outdoors or indoors?

4 What exercises/sports have you enjoyed in the past?

5 Do you know what facilities there are for sports and exercising in your area? If not, where can you find out?

6 How far will you have to travel to do your chosen exercise or sport?

7 What moods and feelings do you associate with exercising?

8 Are you easily bored?

Reflecting on your answers will help you devise a personal exercise plan that suits you. If you don't have much time to exercise, choose an activity that you can easily fit into your everyday life—walking is a sensible and enjoyable way of doing this.

break. The variation need not just be in the exercise you choose; you should also vary the way you perform your chosen sport or exercise. For example, if you like walking you could go on a hike walking slowly over a long distance, but on another occasion you could walk a short distance as fast as possible. Use the environment to increase or decrease intensity: walk up hills, take steps two at a time.

TAKE IT GENTLY

■ Always warm up for five to ten minutes before you begin exercising to increase your circulation and loosen your muscles and joints in preparation for more intense activity. This will help you get the most out of your exercise, prevent post-exercise aches and stiffness, and reduce the risk of injury.

■ Most organized exercise or dance classes will involve a warm-up as part of the class, but if you are exercising alone the easiest way is to walk slowly or march on the spot for five to ten minutes and then do some light stretches.

■ Alternatively, start your exercise session slowly. For example, if you are swimming, start swimming up and down the pool very slowly for five minutes; if you are going for a run, start by walking and gradually speed up until you break into a run.

■ Slow down gradually too to allow your heart rate to return to normal. Wait until you feel comfortable with your exercise regime before adding more days.

■ Take time to learn the basics of any new activity. If you're finding it difficult to keep

up in a class or sport it is probably because you haven't mastered the basics.

■ If you don't have access to a health club, gym, or local trainer, look for books and videos and take it slowly.

■ If you have started a new activity like tennis or dance and discover that your skill level needs to be fairly well developed before you can enjoy it, then switch to something you can do without having to learn a lot of complicated moves, such as cycling or walking.

THE RIGHT ACTIVITY FOR YOU

Activity	What it involves	Pros and cons
Aerobic machines	Machines which simulate various fitness activities, e.g. climbing stairs, walking, skiing, rowing.	Available in most gyms, can be adjusted to your individual fitness level. Can be boring.
Aquaerobics	Aerobic exercise to music in water.	Low-impact because the water takes the strain. Fun. However, resistance of the water can make it difficult to work at a high intensity.
Cardiofunk	Aerobic exercise to funky dance music.	Low-impact. Fun. However, can be hard to follow especially in a big class. Some moves can jar the back.
Cardiosculpting aerobics	A type of low-impact aerobics which involves some standing leg exercises.	The hip and thigh work helps sculpt muscles and improve shape.
Circuit training	Various muscle exercises, e.g. squats, push-ups and other body-conditioning moves together with aerobic activities.	Varied. Fun. Gives all-over workout.
Body conditioning	Traditional floor exercises designed to sculpt and tone underused muscles, e.g. leg lifts, squats, push-ups.	Helps you firm up. However, no cardiovascular benefits so must be combined with aerobic activity.
Cycling	Low-impact aerobic activity.	Varied. Helps develop strong legs and is fat burning. Good if you like being outdoors. Make sure bike is adjusted to your height, otherwise you could risk back and knee problems.
Dancing	Many different forms. Choose from funky disco, exotic Arabian, sedate ballroom, retro Rock n' Roll, fiery flamenco, cool jazz, or trendy Latin.	Helps develop endurance and stamina, cardiovascular, strengthens legs. Varied. Sociable. Fun.
Golf		Calorie burning. Stress relieving.

THE RIGHT ACTIVITY FOR YOU

Activity	What it involves	Pros and cons
High-impact aerobics	Aerobic activities with jumps, running and moves where feet leave the floor.	Cardiovascular. However, can cause injury. Should be done on sprung wooden floor. Pay attention to shoes. Limit to two to three times a week. Avoid if you have back, knee or ankle problems.
Low-impact aerobics	Aerobic activities which avoid both feet leaving floor at the same time.	Good for anyone with back, knee or ankle problems. However, can contain injury risks. Excessive arm movements can cause back and shoulder pain.
Martial arts	Many different types including Karate, Tai Kwon Do, Aikido.	Provides an excellent overall workout. Improves co-ordination. Some moves may stress joints.
Pilates	A method of stretching and body conditioning using floor exercises and apparatus.	Helps increase strength in inner thighs and abdominals. Increases flexibility. Helps reduce stress because it requires concentration and control.
Rackets	Racket game.	Very intense aerobic workout. Good if you thrive on competition. Can cause injury if you have joint or back problems.
Rebounding	Exercising on a mini-trampoline.	Low-impact. Aerobic. Gentle. Can be done at home. Good to get you into exercise if you are unfit.

Activity	What it involves	Pros and cons
Rowing	Using a canoe or rowing machine.	Good for endurance, upper body and legs. Can make back problems worse. Can be done outdoors or indoors using a rowing machine.
Running/jogging	Running or jogging at a slower pace.	Develops leg strength and aerobic fitness. Can be done outdoors or indoors on a treadmill. Safe and natural but can cause injury if you have joint problems.
Slide aerobics	Lateral sliding movements done using a smooth plastic board.	Low-impact. Good for heart, lungs and legs. But can overstress knee joints if you don't have right technique.
Swimming	Swimming in sea or in indoor or outdoor pool.	Good for posture, flexibility and muscle tone. Safe. Water is soothing so good for combating stress.
Video workouts	General fitness workout to a video.	Good all-over workout. Can be repetitive and therefore boring. Go for one led by qualified fitness instructor.
Walking	Walking outside	Low-impact. Easy on joints. Cardiovascular. Fat burning, low intensity. You have to walk for a long time to obtain benefits.

Note: always choose an activity that you can enjoy doing, then you will look forward to your exercise sessions and can build them easily into your normal routine. If you miss a session, for whatever reason, you may feel frustrated and even stressed. If you don't enjoy an activity, there's no point in persevering with it—just try a different activity. For example, you may not like solitary activities, such as running or cycling, but you might find group-oriented dancing or a competitive sport such as tennis, more stimulating and relaxing. These activities provide the opportunity to make new friends and to exercise with other people, encouraging and motivating each other.

STRETCH OUT YOUR STRESS

Stretching is one of the best ways to ease stress as it eases muscle tension and releases endorphins. The best type of stretching is known as static stretching and involves moving slowly into a stretch and holding it. It is the safest technique for stretching as any pain or discomfort can be instantly alleviated by moving out of the stretch. Static stretching is also an ideal way to warm up and help you stay flexible.

Do the following stretches for five to ten minutes before and after exercising. Do each stretch gently and try to relax the muscles being stretched. Feel the stretch in the bulky part of the muscle rather than toward its end at the joints. Do not bounce or force the muscles as you will cause the muscle fiber to contract. If it hurts, then stop. Hold each stretch for about 10 to 30 seconds.

STRETCH YOUR NECK

1 Stand with feet a comfortable distance apart. Keeping your shoulders down and relaxed, gently drop your head to your chest. Hold until you feel the stretch in the back of your neck and the tension starting to ease.

2 Lift your head again. Now tilt your head gently to the right. Hold for five seconds, then repeat on left side allowing your head to roll gently to the left.

■ **Note:** throughout this exercise move slowly and with control. Don't jerk your head or overstretch your neck muscles.

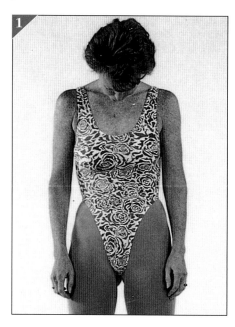

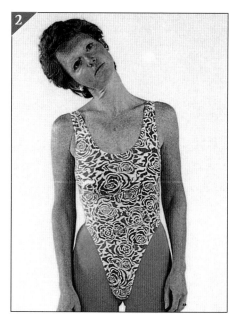

STRETCH YOUR SHOULDERS

Stand with feet a comfortable distance apart. Bring one arm across chest and gently pull with other arm until you feel your shoulder joint stretch. Hold. Change arms.

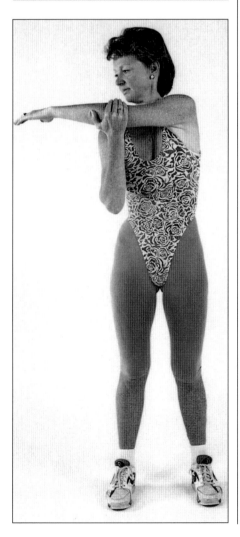

STRETCH YOUR TORSO

Stand with feet shoulder-width apart. Keeping knees soft and slightly bent, reach forward with your left arm, palm facing upward, and stretch your right arm upward toward the ceiling. Feel your ribs lift away from your hips and your spine lengthening. Hold the stretch until you feel your muscles relax. Repeat the stretch on the opposite side.

STRETCH YOUR UPPER BACK

Standing with feet apart, clasp hands in front of your body and stretch arms in front of chest. With one palm on back of the other, press them forward until you feel your shoulder blades separate. Hold.

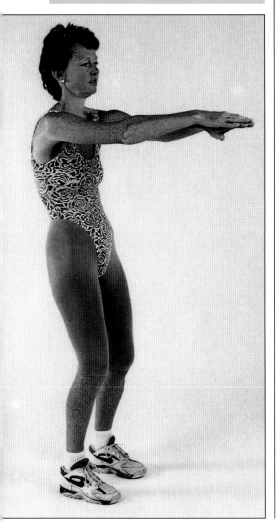

STRETCH YOUR CHEST

Take your arms behind your body and press them away from your back. Press your chest forward.

STRETCH YOUR CALVES

Starting with your feet together, place one leg behind the other and press the heel to the floor. Bend your front leg and lean forward from the hips, pulling your abdominal muscles in tightly. Hold, then repeat on the other side.

STRETCH YOUR HAMSTRINGS

Stand with your feet wide apart and your right leg in front of your body, your left leg back and slightly bent. Place your hands on the upper part of the front thigh and lean your body forward, keeping your ribs lifted and your abdomen pulled in. Feel the stretch along the back of the thigh. Repeat on the other side.

STRETCH YOUR TRICEPS

Take one arm over your head and bend the elbow until your hand is touching between your shoulder blades. With your other hand, hold the front of your elbow and gently press against it to create resistance. When you feel the stretch, hold it, and then repeat on the other side.

STRETCH YOUR INNER THIGHS

With your feet wide apart and toes pointing forward, bend your left knee and straighten your right leg. Keep your body upright and support both hands on your thigh. Hold until you feel the stretch. Then change sides.

STRETCH THE FRONT OF YOUR THIGHS

Stand on one leg, grasping the foot of the other leg with your hand, with the opposite arm pointing forward for balance. Gently pull on your foot until you feel the stretch in your thigh. Hold and repeat on the other side.

STRETCH YOUR TORSO

Stand tall and stretch both arms above your head. Reach for the ceiling with alternate hands, feeling the stretch down the side of your torso to your waist.

STRENGTHEN YOUR OUTER THIGH

Above: lie on your side on the floor, with your bottom leg bent, supporting yourself with your arms. Raise your upper leg, keeping it straight with your foot flexed. Raise and lower the leg. Do this exercise before an aerobic session.

STRENGTHEN YOUR ABDOMEN

Below: lie on the floor, knees bent, feet hip width apart. Place hands on either side of your head. Lift your head, using the muscles in your abdomen. Hold for a few seconds without straining. Lower yourself to the ground. This is another good strengthening exercise.

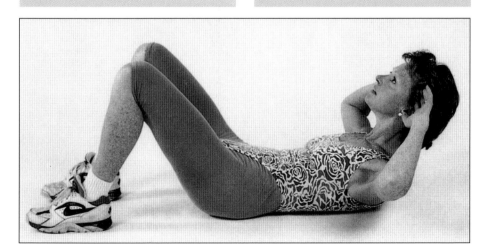

OTHER EXERCISES

Running, gentle jogging, or
walking help you to warm up.
Aim to start by doing 15 minutes
once a week and then gradually
increase your exercise activity
until you are doing 30 minutes
twice or three times a week.

AEROBIC EXERCISES

Joining an aerobic class can be fun as
well as keeping you fit. Aerobic exercise is
good for the heart and helps build up
bones which helps to prevent the brittle
bone disease osteoporosis.

INTRODUCTORY FOUR-WEEK PLAN

If you haven't exercised for a long time try the following gentle four-week plan to get you going. Always listen to your body and if you feel pain or tiredness don't push yourself.

WEEK 1

Sunday:	gentle aerobic exercise, e.g. walking, swimming 15 minutes
Monday:	stretch 15 minutes
Wednesday:	relaxation/meditation/visualization 15 minutes
Friday:	mind-body exercise, e.g. yoga, T'ai chi, Pilates

WEEK 3

Sunday:	mind/body 20 minutes
Tuesday:	gentle aerobic exercise 20 minutes
Thursday:	relaxation/meditation/visualization 20 minutes
Friday:	stretching 20 minutes
Saturday:	gentle aerobic exercise 20 minutes

WEEK 2

Sunday:	stretch 15 minutes
Tuesday:	gentle aerobic exercise 15 minutes
Thursday:	relaxation/meditation/visualization 15 minutes
Saturday:	gentle aerobic exercise 15 minutes

WEEK 4

Sunday:	gentle aerobic exercise 20 minutes
Monday:	relaxation/meditation/visualization 20 minutes
Tuesday:	stretching 20 minutes
Thursday:	mind-body 20 minutes
Saturday:	gentle aerobic exercise 20 minutes

Note: gradually increase the amount of time you spend on each activity by five minutes every two weeks to a total of 30 minutes.

4

RELAXATION TECHNIQUES

Relaxation is just as vital as exercise in stress management. It is a physical skill which can help you to overcome physical, emotional, and mental stress. By learning to relax you can gain control over your autonomic nervous system, which controls vital activities, such as breathing, heart rate, and blood pressure. During deep relaxation, breathing becomes slower, the body uses oxygen more efficiently, the heart beats more slowly and regularly, and the brain emits the slow alpha waves that are associated with meditation.

Learning to relax means becoming aware of when your body needs to stop and take a break. Busy people often find it difficult or impossible to slow down when there is a lull in daily activity. When you have an urgent job to do it's tempting to keep pushing yourself until you have finished it. However, by doing this you are putting yourself on the road to burn-out. Taking a short break to stop and let go from time to time helps you clear your mind and lifts stress and tension. This helps to release stress, harness energy, and makes you function more effectively.

Relaxation is more than just sleeping or flopping down on the sofa in front of the TV. Even small things, such as tapping your fingers, fiddling with your hair, chewing your lip, or sitting with your arms folded rigidly across your body, are all signs of hidden tension and stress. Relaxation means consciously choosing to enter a state of passive awareness and to still the mental chatter and worries of everyday life. And, as with any skill, it demands time and practice. However, once you have learnt how to relax you will be able to do so at will. Just being able to do so for a few minutes restores your body and your mind, enabling you to think more clearly.

Left and opposite: quiet moments of meditation can help you to relax and reduce your stress levels.

RELAXATION TECHNIQUES

There are many different techniques of relaxation, some of which are featured below. But as a first step, try becoming aware of your body and the physical sensations you experience when you are going about everyday activities; for example, making your bed or sweeping the floor can help you to relax, by calming your mind. When you perform such tasks, become aware of your body and the muscles you are using: the stretch in your back when bending to make the bed, the way you stand when you sweep the floor, the strength in your buttocks as you pick up a child, the stretch in your arms as you put something on a high shelf, the feel of your body as you walk upstairs.

PROGRESSIVE RELAXATION

This relaxation technique is very easy to learn. It involves becoming aware of each part of your body in turn and focusing on the feelings of tension, and then consciously releasing them to attain a state of complete relaxation. Use it to help you drop off on those nights when you are lying in bed wide awake with thoughts buzzing around your head.

■ Lie still and breathe slowly and quietly for a few moments.

■ Clench your toes as tightly as you can for a few seconds, then gradually release them. As you do so, mentally say "Relax" to yourself.

■ Move up to your knees and tighten them

as hard as you can. Hold, then let go, again repeating "Relax."

■ Now tighten your thighs. Make them as hard as you can. Then release and "Relax."

■ Now move on to your buttocks. Clench them together as tightly as you can. Hold and "Relax."

■ Pull in your abdomen and tighten it. Hold and "Relax."

■ Pull your shoulders up to your ears. Hold them tightly, then release again, mentally saying "Relax."

■ Clench your fists and tighten your arms and elbows so they are locked and rigid. Hold and then release and "Relax."

■ Squeeze your facial muscles as tightly as you can. Hold, then relax. Feel your mouth become soft, and part your lips slightly. Feel your cheeks, your forehead, your scalp relax. Again, mentally say "Relax."

■ Remain relaxed and breathe slowly and easily.

THE IMPORTANCE OF BREATHING

An important aspect of relaxation is the awareness and control of your breathing. Practitioners of yoga and other Eastern therapies have long claimed that the way we breathe is an important factor in the way we feel. The air we breathe is said to contain *prana*, or vital energy, and the various yogic breathing techniques are known as *pranayama*. There are three different types of breathing (opposite).

THE DIFFERENT LEVELS OF BREATHING

Abdominal breathing (right)

Inhale slowly and deeply. Let your abdomen swell as you breathe in and it fills with air. Then breathe out and, as you do so, draw your abdomen in smoothly and slowly. While you do this, keep your chest and your shoulders still.

Clavicular breathing

Now hold your abdomen and rib cage still and breathe in and out, allowing your shoulders to rise up and down.

Thoracic breathing (below)

Holding your shoulders and your abdomen still, breathe in and expand your rib cage. Breathe out, slowly releasing your ribs and feeling them relax as you do so. Place your palms on your chest and feel your ribs move in and out.

The different breathing types are:

■ Abdominal, or deep, breathing.

■ Thoracic breathing, from the chest.

■ Clavicular breathing, light, rapid breathing from the base of the neck.

Animals and humans when they breathe naturally use all three types of breathing so all the muscles involved are exercised. However, when we are stressed we have a tendency to breathe too shallowly from the top of our lungs. The result is that the muscles involved in abdominal breathing are under-used and weaken. Scientifically, shallow breathing deprives the body of oxygen and stops carbon monoxide wastes from being expelled. This, in turn, causes fatigue. Equally damaging is hyperventilation (fast, shallow breathing from the chest triggered by anxiety) because it saturates the lungs with oxygen and triggers stress hormones, which, in turn, cause exhaustion.

Slower, deeper breathing helps move you into a calmer frame of mind which allows you to attain control over your emotions. Deep breathing helps increase the number of negative ions in the body (charged particles in the air which have a positive effect on the body). Simply becoming aware of the way you breathe and concentrating on taking slow, calm deep breaths helps ground you in the present, banishing irritating and stressful thoughts. At the same time the increased oxygen in the bloodstream helps you feel more energetic and able to meet challenges. Learn to be aware of the different types of breathing by doing the following exercises.

BREATHING EXERCISES

Once you have become aware of the different levels of breathing you can use various breathing exercises to help you relax. Try a few of them and find the ones that suit you best.

■ **Slow, deep breathing**

Try this simple exercise to calm your mind and generate energy whenever you are feeling stressed.

1 Sit comfortably cross-legged on a cushion or on a chair, back straight, hands loosely resting in your lap or on your thighs, forefingers and thumb touching.

2 Close your eyes and become aware of your breathing. Breathe in through the nose filling your lungs from bottom to top and letting your abdomen expand. Rest your hands lightly on your abdomen and feel it rising as you breathe in and falling as you breathe out.

3 Exhale, emptying your lungs from top to bottom, feeling your abdomen relax. Pause slightly between breaths. If you find that your mind is wandering, just return your thoughts to your breath.

4 Try to find the natural rhythm of your breathing so the in-breath is the same length as your out-breath and feel yourself relaxing. Continue to breathe easily for five to 15 minutes.

CREATE YOUR OWN AURA

The next breathing exercise is designed to help buffer you from stress. It is based on a yoga breathing technique.

1 Sit comfortably cross-legged on a

cushion or on a chair with your back straight and concentrate on your breathing. Close your eyes and take a few deep, calming breaths in and out.

2 As you breathe in, imagine your breath flowing up the right-hand side of your body, and as you breathe out imagine your breath flowing down the left side. In your mind's eye imagine your breath circulating all round your body.

3 As you continue to breathe, imagine your breath as your favorite color or as a stream of light and feel it flowing around your body, soothing and calming you.

4 Still visualizing your breath as a stream of light or color on each out-breath, imagine it

surrounding you with a protective aura which buffers you from the effects of stress.

5 Carry on for as long as you feel comfortable, and when you feel perfectly relaxed gradually become aware of the world around you again.

6 When you feel ready, get up and go about your daily business again, but still imagine your protective aura around you.

Below: when we are stressed we often breathe shallowly, creating a build up of carbon dioxide which depletes us of energy. Learning to breathe properly is energizing because it helps calm your body and your mind, and releases stress.

 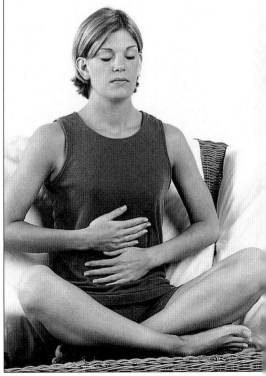

ALTERNATE NOSTRIL BREATHING

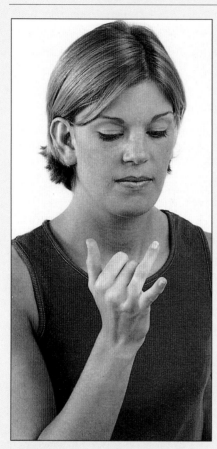 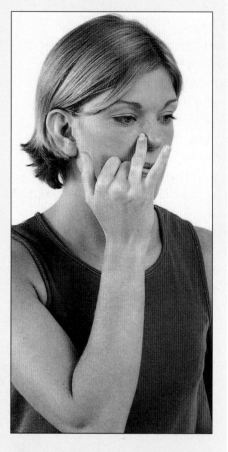

This is another technique culled from yoga which helps calm your thoughts.

1 Sit comfortably cross-legged on a cushion or with your back straight on a chair. Your neck and head should be in a straight line with your spine, your shoulders slightly back and relaxed.

2 Breathe slowly and easily. Try to make the in-breath and the out-breath the same length. Do this for a few seconds until you have established a natural easy rhythm.

3 Tuck the first and second fingers of your right hand into your palm, extending your thumb and fourth and fifth fingers.

4 Breathe out and in through your left nostril only. Now press your right nostril closed with the fourth and fifth fingers and continue to breathe out and in through your left nostril, keeping your breathing slow, even, deep and quiet.

5 Repeat several times.

6 Change sides and repeat the exercise, breathing through your right nostril.

RELAX WITH YOGA

The Indian yoga teacher Patanjali, writing 2,000 years ago, described yoga as "the science of the mind," and today the techniques of yoga are becoming increasingly popular as a way of easing mental and physical stress. The word yoga actually means "union," and practicing it regularly helps to lift stress in several ways.

The various postures, known as *asanas*, help relax and tone your muscles and massage the internal organs. You don't need to be especially supple or fit to carry them out as they can be adapted to allow for any physical injury or weakness. Yoga also uses mental techniques designed to help you concentrate and still the mind. These include the co-ordinated breathing techniques of *pranayama* and also meditation. The various techniques strengthen and complement each other. Stretching your muscles in the *asanas* releases muscular tension and helps you to relax; while calming the mind and releasing buried emotions helps your mind and body to attain a state of detachment which restores balance and banishes stress.

YOGA GUIDELINES

■ It's important to practice yoga every day, so plan a regular time—for example, before breakfast or dinner.

■ You should always practice yoga on an empty stomach.

■ Perform each pose slowly and become aware of the sensations in your body as you do each one.

■ Feel the stretches, and the changes in pressure and become aware of your breathing as you do each pose.

■ Let yourself relax into the postures as you breathe out and hold the position you reach as you breathe in.

■ Don't strain to achieve the final position; find what you feel comfortable with and gently try to increase it from there.

STANDING ASANAS

In yoga, as in many Eastern philosophies, the body is seen as being made up of male and female energy. Standing asanas make use of the male energy which, like the sun, is invigorating, stimulating, and creative. The standing asanas help strengthen your muscles, improve your balance, and discharge energy.

1 Stand with your hands by your sides and fingers outstretched. Breathe in and raise your left arm over your head. Stretch upward and as you breathe out bend from your waist toward the right, sliding your right hand down your thigh. Hold the position and breathe normally. Breathe in again as you return to the upright. Stretch upward, then breathe out and slowly lower your arm. Repeat on the other side.

2 Standing, again slide your hands up to your waist and rest them on your hips, fingers pointing forward. Breathe in and slowly bend backward from the middle of your body, stretching your head and neck back. Feel the stretch in your back. Hold for as long as is comfortable, breathing normally. Gradually return to an upright position and relax your arms to your sides.

3 Standing upright, raise your arms until they are horizontal and pointing out to the sides. Place your feet about shoulder width apart and move your left foot so it is pointing out to the side. Breathe out and bend to the left, sliding your left hand down your leg toward your foot and taking care not to lean forward or backward. At the same time, raise your right arm up, palm facing forward, and look up at your right hand. Hold, stretching a little further each time you breathe out. Breathing out, return to your starting position. Repeat on the other side.

PRONE ASANAS

Use these postures to help ease a stiff spine, stretch your abdomen, and strengthen your back muscles.

1 Lying face down with your legs together, place your hands flat on the floor on either side of your chest. Breathing in, raise your head and breathe out. Breathing in again, raise your chest using your back muscles until your ribs are off the floor. Breathe out. Breathing in again, reach further up and back. Stop just before your belly button comes off the floor. Supporting

yourself on your hands, hold as you breathe out and in three times. Slowly return to the face-down position as you breathe out. This position is called the cobra.
Note: avoid it if you have a hernia or suffer from high blood pressure.

2 Lying face down with your feet together, bend your knees, and bring your feet toward your head. Grasp your ankles with your hands and, breathing in, pull on your feet to raise your thighs, chest and head off the floor. Raise your upper and lower body as much as you can so you are resting on your abdomen. Keep your elbows straight. Feel the stretch along your back. Hold for three breaths and release your legs as you breathe out. This posture is called the bow.
Note: avoid if you have a hernia, suffer from high blood pressure, heart disease, or lower back pain.

SUPINE ASANAS

These postures make use of the body's female energy which is calming, nurturing, and gentle.

1 Lie on your back and, breathing in, raise your legs. Breathing out, raise your legs still further until your hips rise off the floor. Support your hips with your hands, resting your weight on your arms, shoulders, and elbows. Breathe out, lift your legs vertically, letting your torso remain at an angle of 45 degrees. Hold, breathing normally, then bend your legs, release arms, and roll out of the pose as you breathe out. **Note:** avoid this posture if you have glaucoma, pressure in the head and neck, if you are overweight, prone to fluid retention, or menstruating.

2 Sit with your legs outstretched and, breathing out, bend back slowly until your head touches the ground, supporting yourself on your elbows. Using your arms as levers, arch your back and neck. Be careful to take the weight on your arms. Hold. Push up with your elbows to release your head and neck and slowly raise your upper body. This pose is known as the fish.
Note: avoid if you have neck problems.

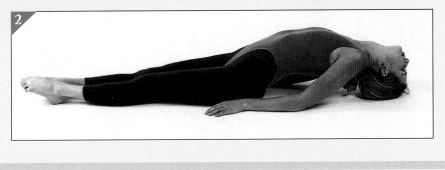

SITTING ASANAS

These postures are particularly calming and relaxing. Start off by sitting on the floor, legs stretched out in front of you. Bend your right leg and tuck the foot under you, then do the same with your left leg, so you are sitting on your insteps. Put a cushion under your buttocks to protect your knees if necessary. Rest your hands on your thighs and sit with a straight back, head balanced and chin tucked in.

1 Kneeling, breathe in and bend back, twisting to the right and placing your right hand on your right heel. Do the same to the left. Arch your back, bringing your head and shoulders back and feeling the stretch in your back. Breathe slowly and evenly for two minutes. Then relax and, breathing out, slide back on your heels. **Note:** you should avoid this posture if you have a hernia or neck or back problems.

2 Sitting with your legs straight in front of you, raise your arms above your head, palms facing forward, and stretch upward from the base of your spine. Breathe in.

3 As you breathe out, bend forward and reach toward your toes, bending from the hips and keeping your back straight. Pull in your abdomen and feel the stretch in your hamstrings. Hold without straining, then relax.

QUICK CALMER

The following quick relaxation routine takes just a few minutes. It uses what is known in yoga as the corpse pose, which involves lying completely relaxed on the floor.

1 Lie down on the floor. Reduce the gap beneath your lower back and the floor by raising your knees to your chest, then sliding your feet along the floor as you lower your legs.

2 Spread your feet about 12 inches apart and spread your arms about 18 inches from your body with palms upward and lightly relaxed. Close your eyes.

3 As you lie on the floor start to focus on your body. Become aware of your abdomen and how it rises and falls as you breathe.

Concentrate on your breathing, noting how it becomes slower and more regular as you observe it. For the next 10 breaths feel your breath flowing into your abdomen as you inhale. Observe how your abdomen fills up like a balloon, then feel it deflate as you exhale. Don't force your breathing; simply observe it.

4 Now feel yourself relax as you exhale and your body sinks into the ground and note the small pause before you inhale and how your body feels light and energetic. Concentrate on these alternate feelings of relaxation and energy as you exhale and inhale 10 times.

5 Get up slowly, feeling more relaxed and energized.

MEDITATION

One of the most effective stress-busters, meditation has been a part of most cultures and religions throughout the ages and the technique lies at the heart of yoga. While many of us have developed the skill of concentration, few of us have the ability to slip into inner peace at will. Meditation is an extremely valuable skill to develop as being able to calm your mind takes your mind away from immediate worries, freeing your unconscious to start to work on helping to solve your problems.

Meditation has a whole range of physical and psychological benefits: our breathing, heart and pulse rates slow and the brain produces long alpha waves which are a sign of deep relaxation. Meditation has important health benefits too, including lifting anxiety, lowering blood pressure, relieving insomnia, panic, premenstrual tension, migraine, asthma, and irritable bowel syndrome. There are many different ways to meditate but all involve four main elements: being in a quiet environment; regulating your breath; becoming physically relaxed; and focusing on an object, thought, word or sound (*mantra*), or an activity that enables the mind to attain a state of relaxed concentration.

PREPARING TO MEDITATE

Before you meditate take a little time to prepare your surroundings.

■ **Temperature** Loosen any tight clothing and make sure the temperature of the room in which you are to meditate is comfortable (neither too hot nor too cold, as both are distracting).

■ **Lighting** Check the lighting: gentle daylight or a dimmed light is ideal. Some people like to light a candle. Avoid sitting in a dark room as you may become drowsy and fall asleep; similarly, avoid bright light as this will strain your eyes.

■ **Posture** Your posture is important. You can either sit in the traditional lotus position (opposite), kneel, or choose a firm chair in which you can sit upright. Place your feet firmly on the ground to keep yourself rooted. Don't meditate lying down or sitting in an armchair, or you will soon drop off. Keep your spine straight and sit in an alert, poised posture.

■ **Breathing** Become aware of your breathing and mentally follow your breath in and out for a few minutes before starting to meditate.

USING A MANTRA

The following meditation based on one used in yoga involves the use of a mantra or sound. Sit with your legs out straight in front of you parted to form a "V"-shape. Bend your right knee and bring your right foot toward you and place it on the floor close to your groin. Bend your left leg and place your left foot on the floor close to your right leg. Rest your hands on your knees. Keep your back straight and breathe slowly and naturally.

Choose a word such as "Om," "One" or "Peace" and chant it inwardly to yourself.

Don't say it out loud or move your lips; just listen to the sound in your mind. Repeat it over and over again, and if any thoughts threaten to intrude let them pass away. When you have established a rhythm, slow down the chanting, but speed it up again if your thoughts threaten to intrude. Once you feel at peace, make your internal sound loudly and deeply and feel an imaginary resonance passing through your body. Start the word slowly and build up to a loud, vibrating sound, then allow to fade gradually into silence. Gradually lengthen

Above: meditation is a very effective technique for managing stress.

the sound until it becomes continuous, ebbing and flowing like a swelling wave that doesn't break. Finally let it ebb away completely and remain in the silent space.

Observe your thoughts and let them pass, but if you are tempted to get caught up in them, start chanting again until they are vanquished. Finish the meditation by beaming good will to those you love, those you know and, finally, all other living things.

CHAPTER FIVE

MASSAGE

Massage is one of the best ways of reducing stress, encouraging relaxation and releasing physical and mental tension. It is wonderful for tackling a whole range of stress-linked problems, such as insomnia, headaches, high blood pressure, depression and anxiety, and it can help ease constipation and muscle strain.

THE MAGIC OF MASSAGE

The sense of touch is as fundamental as breathing and its power to relax, invigorate, and soothe is second to none. Think how you instinctively rub your temples if you have a headache, or your eyes when you are tired. Babies in the womb develop the ability to feel before any other. Ultrasound scans reveal that they flinch from an unpleasant sensation, such as a needle, but relax and quieten if the abdomen is stroked. After birth the sense of touch provides a bridge from the baby to the world, long before a child is able to speak. Perhaps this is why, as adults, being touched can induce an almost instant feeling of security and comfort.

EFFECTS OF MASSAGE

Massage can have profound physical effects on you.
■ It boosts the circulation.

■ It lowers blood pressure.
■ It aids digestion.
■ It relaxes muscles.
■ By stimulating the body's lymphatic system, it speeds up the disposal of toxins from the body.

At the same time, the feelings of well-being brought about by massage trigger the release of endorphins— the body's pain-

WHEN NOT TO MASSAGE

Massage is not advisable in the following situations:
■ Specific skin problems, such as bad eczema and psoriasis.
■ Swelling or inflammation affecting part of the body.
■ Severe injury or back pain.
■ In the first three months of pregnancy.
■ If someone is undergoing medical or psychiatric treatment (only on medical advice).
■ Serious illnesses, such as cancer, HIV, and after surgery (unless agreed by the doctor).
■ Where there is tissue damage or weakness, such as a recently broken bone, inflammation, or varicose veins, direct pressure over the spot should be avoided.

relieving hormones. These physical effects, combined with the psychological benefits of being touched and feeling cared for, produce a tremendous feeling of release and relaxation. There are many different types of massage. In some, which are often described as therapeutic or remedial, the strokes used can be quite vigorous, even somewhat painful—a sign that tension is being released. In other types, for instance, aromatherapy, the very lightest of gentle strokes may be used. However, whatever the type of massage, a number of basic techniques are used (see the chart opposite).

Below: massage helps ease out stress in the shoulders, one of the commonest sites in the body for tension to be held.

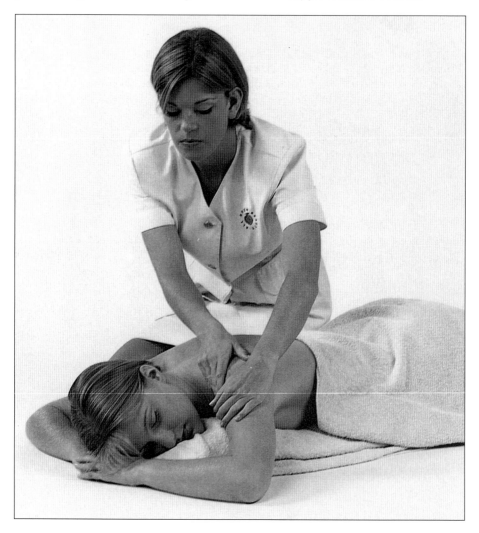

THE BASIC STROKES

Stroke	Description	How it is done	Useful for
Effleurage	A long stroking movement which allows the therapist to initiate contact with the body.	Using either flat or cupped hands, glide over the skin with a constant even pressure, using slow and gentle circular movements. Apply pressure on the upward stroke with light pressure on the return.	Warms and relaxes the body, stimulating circulation and lymph flow. Flat-hand effleurage can be used for large flat surfaces, e.g. the back, in preparation for deeper work. Cupped-hand effleurage can be used on the calves and thigh muscles.
Petrissage	Rhythmic lifting, squeezing, and rolling of the muscles with the hands.	Grasp the flesh between thumb and fingers and pull it, using firm movements to pull the body as well as the muscles. Use either two hands to squeeze the muscle in opposite directions, or rest one hand lightly on the body while squeezing with the other, using the heel of the hand to apply pressure.	Pumping nutrients through the muscles and draining away wastes at the same time as acting on the deeper blood and lymph vessels.
Wringing	As the name suggests, the flesh is wrung between two hands.	Work the hands in opposite directions as if slowly wringing out a towel.	To ease muscle tension in the legs and thighs. On the thigh, keep the thumb and fingers together; on the calf, spread the thumb wide to get a good grip on the muscle.
Kneading	The flesh is squeezed between thumb and fingers rather like kneading dough. It is used with wringing.	Slightly lean into the flesh as you lift and squeeze it to avoid pinching.	Slow deep movements help calm and relax and ease congestion in the tissues. Quicker movements can be used to stimulate energy. Used on fleshy areas, e.g. the thighs and buttocks. Never knead over varicose veins or broken blood vessels.

THE BASIC STROKES

Stroke	Description	How it is done	Useful for
Circular knuckling	The hands are rotated in a circular movement over the area being massaged.	Curl your hands into loose fists with the middle part resting against the body, and make circular movements without moving your hands over the flesh.	Releasing tension on the upper chest and shoulders.
Tapotement or percussion	Cupping, slapping, and chopping with the hands.	The wrists should be loose and flexible and movements fast and invigorating but not painful. You can use loosely curled fists to pound fleshy areas, e.g. the thighs and buttocks, or the side of the hands to hack with a chopping movement.	Improving muscle tone, firming sagging skin, boosting blood flow, and releasing tension.
Circling	Circular rotation with the fingertips over the area being massaged.	Place one hand on top of the other with fingers straight but relaxed. Press into the muscle with your fingertips and rotate them in slow, small circles.	Easing any muscle that needs deep pressure, e.g. the back, tops of the shoulders, calves, and the muscles on either side of the spine.
Friction	Rapid oscilating movements over the flesh being massaged.	Place the palms of your hands on the body and use even pressure to rub them backward and forward energetically with firm movements.	Increasing the blood supply to internal organs and easing stiff joints.

Right: always warm your hands and the massage oil, if using, before starting the massage.

SELF-MASSAGE

Learning to massage yourself enables you to ease feelings of stress at any time. Wherever you are, you can use a few simple strokes to ease tension, stimulate circulation and even treat minor ailments. You can massage yourself at home, at work, or while you are traveling. For example, at work the face and hands can become taut and tense, especially if you use a VDU. A simple 10-minute self-massage can help to ease eyestrain and relax stiff hands and wrists that can lead to repetitive strain injury.

Self-massage isn't new. In fact, in some Eastern countries the techniques are handed down in families, and it is even sometimes taught in schools. Below, you will find a number of simple massages that you can do. Some can be done whenever you have a few moments spare. No special preparation, equipment or oils are needed. However, if you do want to set aside some more time to do some self-massage, it will be more beneficial and it's a good way to feel pampered.

FACE

■ **To lift headaches and alleviate eyestrain**
Rest your fingers on your temples, letting them take the weight of your neck. Then, using the two middle fingers, apply small circular fingertip pressure in a clockwise direction.

FACE

A simple face massage will ease tension, soothe away anxiety and help to alleviate eye strain.

■ **To release taut muscles and rest overworked eyes**
Sit down and rest your elbows on a table or desk, then cup your hands over your eyes. Hold for approximately 30 seconds. Now bring the heels of the hands to eyebrow level and glide them across your brows to your temples until you reach your hairline. Perform this simple massage whenever you feel stressed or your eyes ache.

FACE

■ **To ease out a concentration frown**
Rub your fingers in a scissor-like action across the middle of your forehead and then out to either side. You can repeat this massage movement slowly when you feel tension in your forehead.

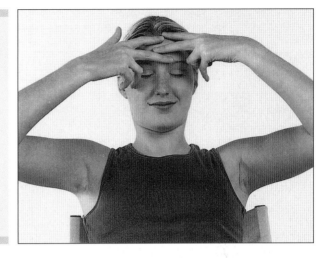

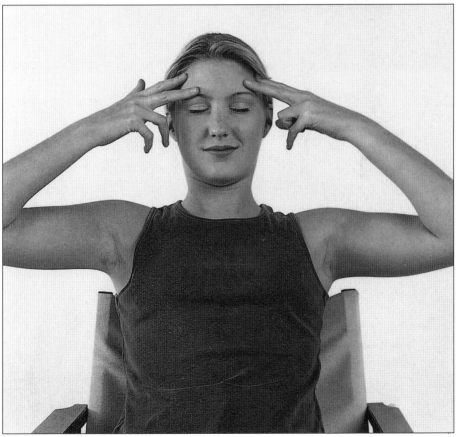

HANDS, ARMS AND WRISTS

■ To relax the hands

Stroke across the palm with the heel of the opposite hand. Glide back and repeat, then do the same working from the fingers to the wrist. Next, stretch the fingers by holding each one at the base and pulling firmly toward you as you work toward the tip, sliding and twisting your grip. When you reach the tip, squeeze and firmly pull each finger, then release.

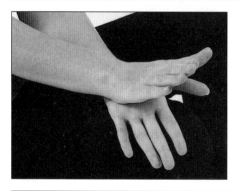

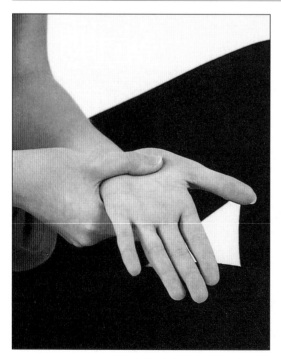

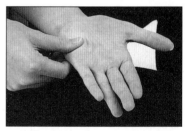

HANDS, ARMS AND WRISTS

■ To ease tension in the palm and relieve headaches

Turn your hand so it is palm upwards and apply circular thumb pressure to the base of the thumb and all over the palm. Concentrate especially on the thick pads of muscles on each side of the palm.

HANDS, ARMS AND WRISTS

■ **To ease tension in your forearm**
Massage your forearm gently with circular thumb pressure. Then gradually move up the arm stroking the whole area right up to the elbow. Repeat this massage on the other hand and arm.

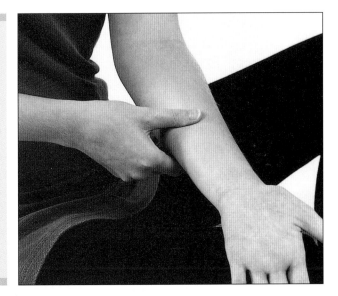

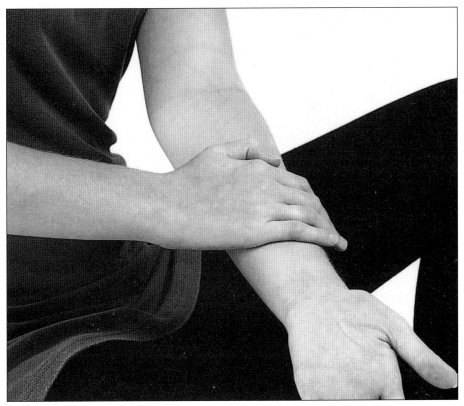

FEET

Tired, aching feet can result in poor posture and even backache. Give weary feet a boost and you will find it revives and refreshes your whole body.

1 Place the heels of your hands on either side of your foot and wrap your fingers underneath. Glide your hands out to the side of your foot, pressing your fingers into the sole to stretch the top of your foot, loosen the muscles, and invigorate the foot. Repeat several times.

2 Rotate the thumbs in a small circle over the top of your foot, leaning into them slightly to increase the pressure and paying special attention to any painful areas.

3 Wrap your hands around your foot and press down with your thumbs.

4 Slide your thumbs up slowly from the gap between each toe to the ankle with firm, rhythmic strokes.

5 Place one palm across the top of your foot and the other underneath, below the toes. Using gentle pressure, make circular movements with both hands.

continued on page 80

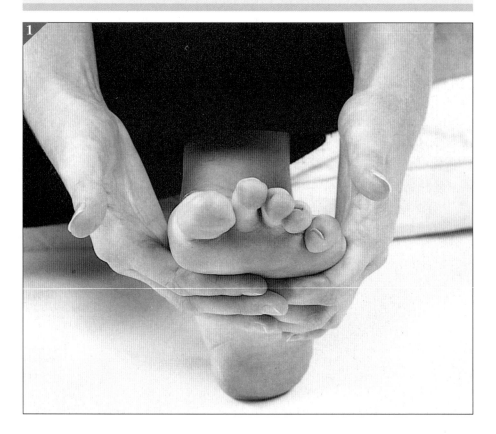

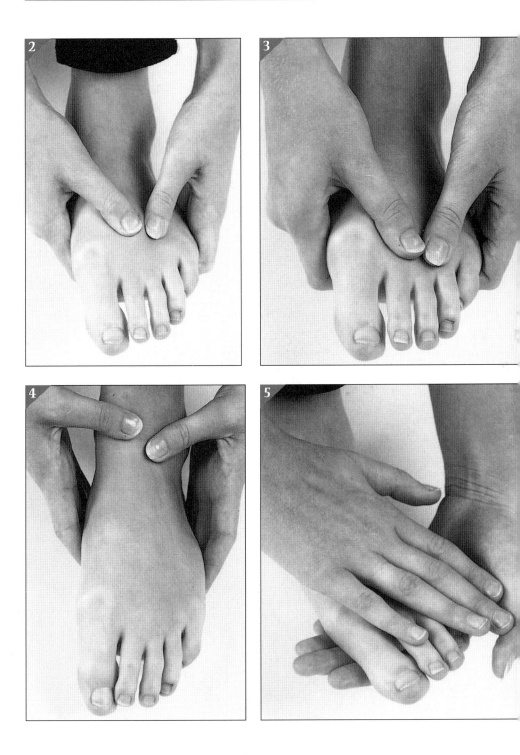

FEET

continued from page 78

6 Pound the sole and sides of your foot with your fists, paying special attention to the heel.

7 Then hack the sole of your foot with the side of your hand. Make sure your wrist and hand are relaxed.

8 Hold the foot between the thumb and fingers of one hand and, using the thumb and index finger of your other hand, squeeze and rotate each toe in turn.

9 Stroke the foot and repeat on the other foot.

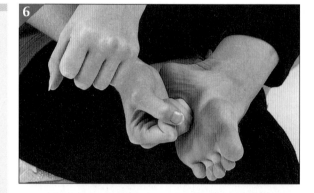

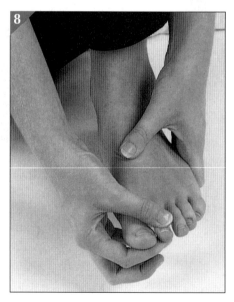

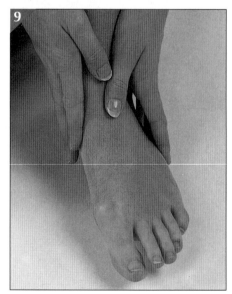

AFTER SPORT AND EXERCISE

Massage hastens the body's recovery from sport and exercise, eases stiffness and cramps, and speeds up the elimination of wastes. These include lactic acid which builds up in the muscles.

1 To relieve calf cramp
Sit with the affected leg straight and the other knee bent. Pull the toes of your straight leg toward you, feeling the stretch in the calf muscle. Hold until the pain starts to ease.

2 To relieve hamstring cramp
Lie on your back and raise the affected leg, keeping the other leg bent. Stroke the back of the thigh firmly with alternate hands.

3 To ease pain and restore muscles after exercise
Using both thumbs, apply deep pressure backward and forward across any tight bands of muscles.

AROMATHERAPY MASSAGE

A smell can evoke a memory more surely than almost anything else. This is because an ancient area of the brain known as the limbus, which is concerned with emotion and memory, lies next to the area that deals with smell. This is the reason why an aromatherapy massage, one of the gentlest and most sensuous forms of massage, is so powerful.

Essential oils, which are extracted from the flowers, seeds, bark, root, and leaves of plants and mixed in a carrier, such as almond oil, are used in the massage. Certain oils are known to work on the psyche, and aromatherapy is useful in treating stress-linked complaints.

Below: mix the essential and carrier oils in the desired proportions, and warm in your hands before using.

USING ESSENTIAL OILS

Choose a carrier oil, such as sunflower, sweet almond, apricot kernel, soya, or grapeseed, and mix with an essential oil from the list overleaf. The normal dilution is the number of millilitres divided by four (e.g. 20ml carrier divided by four equals maximum five drops essential oil).

However, for sensitive skin or during pregnancy you will need a more diluted mixture so divide the number of millilitres by six (e.g. 20ml carrier divided by six equals three drops essential oil). If you have very sensitive skin, use one drop of essential oil per 10ml of carrier or use sweet almond oil alone.

SAFETY TIPS

■ Always dilute essential oils.
■ Before using a new oil, place a diluted drop on your inner wrist. Apply a plaster and check after 12 hours. If it irritates, do not use the oil.
■ Never take essential oils internally.
■ If you are pregnant or have a medical condition, consult your doctor and a qualified aromatherapist before using essential oils.

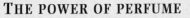

THE POWER OF PERFUME

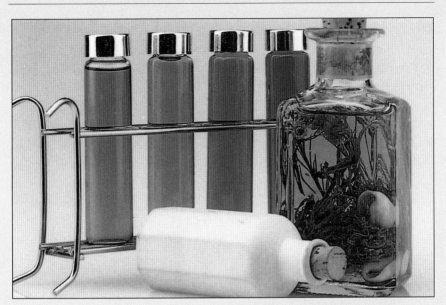

■ **Chamomile**
Helps ease insomnia and calms emotional upsets, soothes muscular pain and headaches.

■ **Clary Sage**
Relaxing. Eases depression, exhaustion, and insomnia. Avoid in pregnancy.

■ **Lavender**
Soothing and sedative. Helps beat insomnia, jetlag, and headaches.

■ **Marjoram**
Sedative. Helps induce sleep. Avoid during pregnancy.

■ **Neroli**
Tranquillizing and relaxing. Useful for insomnia, PMS, irritable bowel syndrome. Avoid sun and sunbeds for six hours as citrus oils increase sensitivity to sunlight.

■ **Rose**
A stimulating oil. Counters lethargy, lifts depression, aids alertness.

■ **Rosemary**
Invigorates and stimulates the central nervous system. Eases headaches, lifts fatigue. Avoid in pregnancy, and if you have high blood pressure or epilepsy.

■ **Sandalwood**
Calming. Lifts depression and anxiety.

AROMATHERAPY FOR STRESS AND TENSION

There are many essential oils which can be used to deal with stress depending on how the stress manifests itself. Geranium, Lavender, Neroli, Rose, and Ylang Ylang help you to relax if you feel tense, irritable, or angry. Meanwhile, Basil, Bergamot, Cinnamon, Geranium, Orange, Rosemary, and Lime are uplifting if you feel tired. Essential oils can be used in many ways.

■ **Inhalations** are made by adding a few drops of the oil to water and inhaling the steam. These are especially good for colds and other respiratory problems.

■ **Compresses** are useful where massage would not be advisable or would be uncomfortable, e.g. after a sprain, torn muscle, or bruise. Some headaches respond

Below: an aromatherapy massage can be relaxing, stimulating or soothing.

well to a cold compress soaked in cold water to which Lavender oil has been added. Period pains can be eased by hot compresses with Marjoram oil.

■ **Baths** Adding oils such as Marjoram and Lavender to a bath is useful for easing insomnia, whereas stimulating oils, such as Rosemary, can help invigorate you.

■ **Vaporizers** Essential oils burnt in a special vaporizer can help calm you down during periods of stress.

■ **Aromatherapy massage** is a combination of techniques from other massage styles which have been adapted to help the body absorb the oils and promote a feeling of well-being.

A healthy body needs healthy cells. Once the oils are absorbed by the skin they pass into tissue fluids, taken into the lymphatic system from where they pass into the bloodstream to be circulated around the body, a process which takes

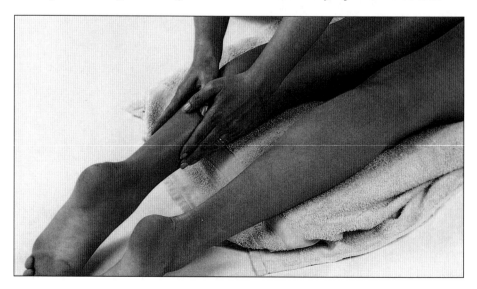

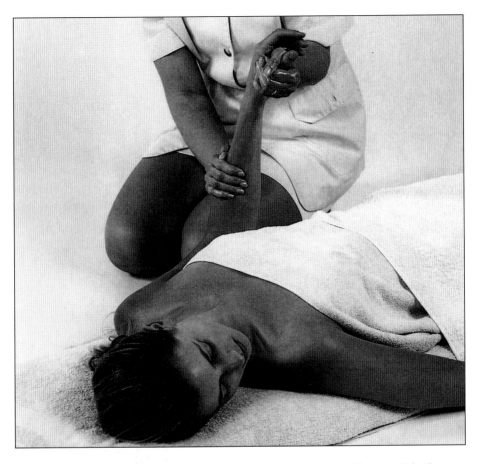

anything from 20 minutes to several days. Certain oils have an affinity for certain organs. For example, Rosemary has an affinity for the liver. When it reaches the liver on its journey around the bloodstream it is dissolved in the tissue fluid, together with other substances the liver needs, such as oxygen and fat-soluble vitamins. The oil contains a number of chemicals that the liver cells require to stay healthy. Other oils are less specific in their effects and act more generally on the tissues to stimulate, cleanse, and tone.

Above: a massage with essential oils helps to promote well-being.

Some essential oils, such as Neroli and Lavender, help promote healthy cell growth; others contain plant hormones to stimulate or rebalance the production of the body's own hormonal system. Fennel, for example, is what is known as a phytestrogen (plant estrogen) so is useful for women's problems such as PMS and the menopause. Effects can làst from several hours to several days.

PUTTING ON THE PRESSURE

The Eastern pressure point techniques, acupressure, which originated in China, and shiatsu, which originated in Japan, are both useful for easing stress and can be easily learnt at home for self-treatment. They work on the same principles as acupuncture by balancing the flow of the body's essential life force, or Chi.

Chi is said to flow to all parts of the body along a system of invisible meridians or energy lines. Pressure on points along these lines is capable of releasing blockages and strengthening or relaxing the internal organs, the spine, and the central nervous system. The therapist working on your fully clothed body exerts pressure with the thumbs, elbows, knees, and feet.

Acupressure and shiatsu are particularly successful in helping ease back pain, period pains, headaches, sleeplessness, fatigue, depression, and muscular tension. Both of these therapies can be used as self-help techniques to relieve headaches, sinus problems, neuralgia, and a whole host of other stress-linked problems.

Below and above left: shiatsu and acupressure can help by unblocking the flow of Chi and rebalancing energy levels so that you feel less stressed.

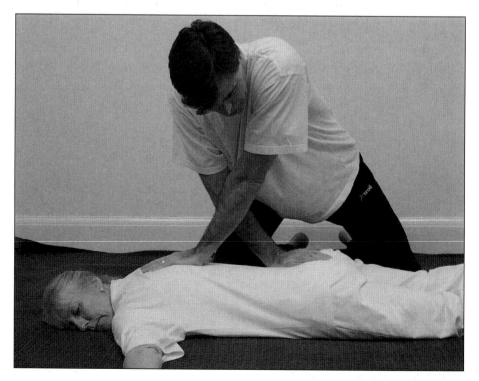

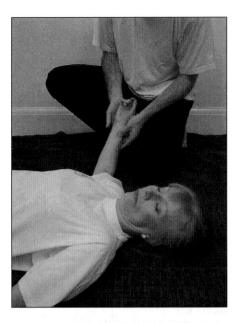

FEET FIRST

Reflexology is a type of acupressure that concentrates on the feet. Practitioners claim that disorders in the rest of the body are reflected by sensitivity in a particular area of the feet. If you imagine the body superimposed on the soles of the feet, the big toe corresponds to the head, the inside edges of the feet to the spine, and the main organs of the body are distributed in approximately the same positions that they are found in the body.

A reflexology massage involves pressing on specific points on the feet to treat the affected areas. It is said to be useful for PMS, migraine, back pain, many digestive problems, and stress-related illnesses. There's no scientific explanation for how reflexology works, as yet, although the feet are rich in nerve endings. However, many reflexologists themselves believe that they are tapping into invisible energy lines, or meridians, in the same way as acupressure.

Above and right: if there is a blockage in the energy flow, crystalline deposits form in the feet. Working on the reflexes in the foot can help rebalance the body.

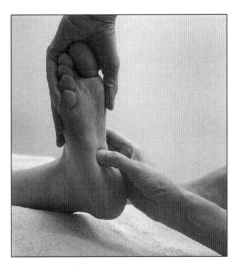

CHAPTER SIX

YOUR STRESS MANAGEMENT PLAN

In this chapter, you will learn how you can put together all the techniques and advice you have received in order to work out a personalized strategy for dealing with stress in your life. There are three steps to creating your own personal stress management plan.

■ **The first** is to analyse the sources of stress in your life so you can learn to anticipate and control it.

■ **The second** is to look at the way you react so you can become aware of when you are feeling stressed and take action to defuse it.

■ **The third** is to make a detailed action plan and start putting it into practice.

ANALYZING YOUR STRESS

Stress, as we have seen, comes from many different sources. Look again at the stress scale (see page 13) to help you to identify major life changes. However, remember that it is not just these major changes that are stressful. Every aspect of your everyday life can add to or subtract from the burden of stress. The following quiz (opposite) is designed to help you to pinpoint potential sources of stress in different areas of your life.

Below: take time to create your own personal stress management plan.

HOW STRESSED ARE YOU?

Answer "Yes" or "No" to the
following questions.

YES NO

Your environment

1 Is your living space small,
cramped, or lacking privacy? ☐ ☐

2 Do you have noisy
neighbors? ☐ ☐

3 Does the winter get you
down? ☐ ☐

4 Do you work or live near
a busy road? ☐ ☐

5 Do you find it hard to relax
at home? ☐ ☐

Your personality

1 Do you feel you have more
faults than good points? ☐ ☐

2 Do you get worked up when
faced with a difficult
situation? ☐ ☐

3 Do you find it hard to relax? ☐ ☐

4 Do you feel you must be
best at everything? ☐ ☐

5 Do you lose your temper
easily? ☐ ☐

Your body

1 Do you often eat quickly or
while you are doing other
things? ☐ ☐

2 Do you regularly eat
convenience foods? ☐ ☐

3 Do you smoke or drink? ☐ ☐

4 Do you neglect your body? ☐ ☐

YES NO

5 Do you often fall prey to
colds or other infections? ☐ ☐

Your relationships

1 Do you feel you never have
enough time for yourself? ☐ ☐

2 Are you going through
relationship problems? ☐ ☐

3 Do you feel you see enough
of your friends? ☐ ☐

4 Do you feel that your life
lacks affection? ☐ ☐

5 Do you often give up things
you want to do because of your
friends or family? ☐ ☐

Your job

1 Do you regularly work
overtime or through your
lunch hour? ☐ ☐

2 Do you feel your abilities are
not fully appreciated at work? ☐ ☐

3 Do you feel you are required
to do to many things at once? ☐ ☐

4 Does your job involve
constant deadlines? ☐ ☐

5 Do you work in a noisy,
stuffy, or smelly atmosphere? ☐ ☐

Continued on page 92

HOW STRESSED ARE YOU? *continued*

YES NO

Your time management

1 Do you often run out of time when you are trying to do something? ☐ ☐

2 Do you often forget appointments or deadlines? ☐ ☐

3 Do you always feel in a hurry? ☐ ☐

4 Do you always travel to work in the rush hour? ☐ ☐

5 Do you spend most of your time with other people? ☐ ☐

Scoring

Score one point for every "yes" answer.

25–30

You are stressed in every area of your life. It is important to tackle this to avoid developing a stress-related illness. Look at the various areas in which you have identified stress and, using the methods outlined in this book, make a plan for dealing with them. It is particularly important when you are under this amount of stress to make sure you make time for exercise and relaxation and pay attention to your own needs, for example, by treating yourself to a professional massage or asking your partner or a friend to massage you. The section on time management in this chapter will give you some suggestions as to how you can organize your time more effectively so as to create space for yourself. It's also vital that you should eat properly so your body is strong and healthy.

10–24

You are moderately stressed at the moment, but this could tip into overstress if you are not careful. Pay particular attention to any areas in which you had a lot of "yeses" and work out ways in which you can ease the burden. Have a look at the tips on managing time and being assertive, and pay attention to healthy eating. Above all, don't forget to build some relaxation and exercise into your life.

0–9

Although there are some areas of stress you don't have too much stress in your life at the moment. However, stress can build up at any time so it's still worth thinking about your life and how to deal with stress when it does occur. The quiz will have identified some areas to which you need to pay special attention if you are to reduce stress. You can use this as the basis for stress-proofing your life.

Opposite: regular exercise, whether it's running, swimming, cycling, working out in the gym, playing competitive sports, or just walking, will help to refresh and revitalize you and to combat the stress in your everyday life. You should try to exercise at least three times a week for 20–30 minutes per session.

RECOGNIZING THE SIGNS

The next part of your individual stress strategy is thinking about how you react to stress and learning to recognize the signs that you are under stress. We all have our individual weak spots which are usually the first to show the signs of stress. The chart that follows is designed to help you identify yours. Becoming aware of the way you react will help you to pick up the first signs of stress so you can change your response accordingly.

Mark each answer on a scale of 1 to 5.

1 Never
2 Very occasionally
3 Sometimes
4 Often
5 All the time

How does stress affect your body?

	1	2	3	4	5
■ Bite your nails					
■ Clench your fists					
■ Drum your fingers					
■ Grind your teeth					
■ Hunch your shoulders					
■ Pick at your skin					
■ Tap your feet					
■ Touch/pull out your hair					

How does stress affect your mood?

	1	2	3	4	5
■ Anxious thoughts					
■ Disturbed sleep					
■ Depression					
■ Irritability					
■ Hostility					
■ Impatience					
■ Restlessness					
■ Helplessness					
■ Hopelessness					
■ Frustration					

	1	2	3	4	5
■ Mind can't stay still					

How does stress affect your behavior?

	1	2	3	4	5
■ Smoking/drinking/ eating/spending more than usual					
■ Finding it difficult to summon up the energy to do anything					
■ Hurling yourself into a round of constant activity					
■ Seeing less of friends					
■ Finding it difficult to get to sleep or stay asleep					
■ Trying to do several things at once					
■ Leaving jobs unfinished					
■ Taking time off work					
■ Speaking more loudly/ quietly than usual					
■ Taking sleeping pills or tranquillizers					
■ Over-reacting to minor problems					

How does stress affect you mentally and emotionally?

	1	2	3	4	5
■ Worrying for no reason					
■ Being more forgetful than usual					
■ Feelings of failure					
■ Finding it difficult to concentrate					
■ Mind racing					

	1	2	3	4	5
■ Panic attacks					
■ Feeling restless					
■ Problems sleeping					
■ Finding it hard to make decisions					
■ Feeling impatient					
■ Loss of interest in things that used to give you pleasure					

Note: when you come to reflect on your answers, you should be able to identify a pattern of personal responses to stress. This will allow you to spot times when you are becoming stressed and help you to plan strategies for dealing with it.

STRESS-PROOFING YOUR LIFE

Realistically it's not always possible to avoid stress. However, you can learn to make it work for you rather than against you. Distressing situations don't always go away. Having a plan of action so problems don't loom so large while, at the same time, doing things that make you feel good about yourself and about life will enable you to attain more of a balance, to feel more in control and less stressed.

THE FIRST STEP

Think about all the sources of stress in your life using the first quiz in this chapter as a basis, and including all the everyday irritations, such as mislaying your check book, that make your life stressful as well as the major upsets. Ask yourself, "What upsets me?" "What makes me feel unhappy?" "What makes me feel stressed?"

Now consider the following ways of dealing with any individual stressor. Can you choose to ignore it? For example, you can choose to ignore the fact that you are always mislaying your check book. If you decide you can't ignore it, is there anything you could do about it?

For example, you could start putting your check book in the top drawer of your desk every time you have used it so you know where to find it. If you don't feel there is anything you can do to change the situation, ask yourself whether there is anything you can do to make it go away, e.g. stop using your check book, and pay your bills straight out of your account? Finally, if you can't avoid it, change it, or make it go away, is there any way you can change your reaction to it? For example, you can decide that there are more things in life to get upset about than losing your check book. Or you can reframe the problem so that it seems funny or silly

Left: try to build some regular exercise into your routine to combat stress.

rather than important. Although the check book example is perhaps trivial, it can be applied to bigger sources of stress.

Try taking one or two items from your list and working them through in this way and you will see how it is possible to defuse stress.

THE SECOND STEP

This is to counterbalance stressful events and situations. Think about what you enjoy doing, what makes you feel enthusiastic, who you enjoy sharing good experiences with. Are there any positive aspects of your life that you are taking for granted or ignoring? Now think about how to inject more of the fun things you have identified into your life, and work out a plan of action for increasing the experiences you find revitalizing. Here are a few suggestions. Add your own.

■ **Get physical** For example, if you are worried about something, go for a swim or a run—and then do what you have to do.

■ **Create something** Paint a picture, write a poem, make a garment, or create a piece of jewelry.

■ **Work it off** If you are fit you can workout, dance, play a hard game of tennis, or whatever to release pent-up energy when you are under stress.

■ **Meditate** As we have seen, this can help to change negative emotions, transforming them into creative ideas.

■ **Treat yourself to something small** Have a bath with essential oils in it, arrange lunch with a friend, talk on the phone to someone you love.

Below: the secret of keeping stress under control is to keep a healthy balance in your life and make sure you do plenty of things you enjoy, including exercise.

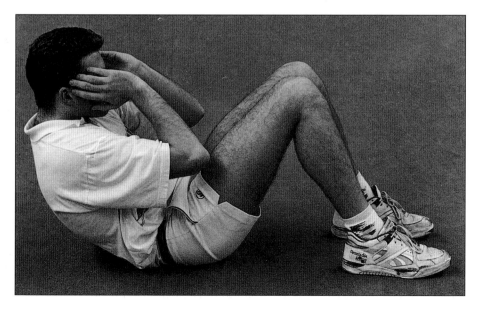

IMPROVING YOUR ENVIRONMENT

Environment and mood are closely linked. Ideally, your home should be a haven where you can retreat from stress.

■ **Space** If your home is cramped or overcrowded it can be a source of stress. However small the space, keeping it clean and tidy will help to make it more comfortable and seem larger. Clutter and untidiness create mental stress. Even if you don't have a separate room you can create some personal space. Try screening off a part of your sitting room or bedroom with a folding screen, a blind, some shelves, or a curtain and use it for relaxation, meditation, or simply spending time alone.

■ **Noise and lighting** These are less easy to control. Heavy drapes or double glazing will help to cut out street noise. Noisy neighbors may need tactful handling. You may want to try using earplugs, or if the noise is really getting you down, find out what your rights are. Many people feel more stressed in winter as a result of SAD—seasonal affective disorder— which is caused by lack of daylight. If this affects you, try to get out in the daylight for as much time as you can every day and install a natural daylight bulb in one of your light fittings at home or at work.

■ **Cheerful decorations** These will also help to lift your mood. Tune into the chemistry of color: blue is calming and stress relieving; yellow can help you feel sunny; violet can bring feelings of inner peace; white can help you empty your mind.

LOOKING BACK

Thinking about how you have dealt with stress in the past can help you to cope with stress in the present and future. Look back to times in your life when you felt under stress and analyse why the situation was stressful. Try to identify the specific factors that cause a situation to be stressful for you. Now try to work out ways to prevent pressure building up again, using some of the suggestions in this book. Recognize that managing stress means considering the whole situation and working to achieve a balance between the various parts of your life. Finally, make a list of ways in which you can prevent such a situation building up again.

HARNESSING THE FEEL-GOOD FACTOR TO FIGHT STRESS

Feeling good about yourself can help you to withstand stress better. The way you look can help you feel better or worse about yourself so take a long hard look at yourself in the mirror. If you aren't happy with what you see, make some changes.

■ Sort through your closet and discard any clothes that you don't feel good in.

■ Make sure your hair, skin, and nails are in good condition.

■ Think about your achievements too and give yourself a pat on the back for a job well done or something achieved.

True health comes from within and it is vital, as we have seen, to make sure you are in good health physically. A varied, healthy diet will ensure that your mind and body

can cope with stress. Read the sections
on diet in Chapter Three and try to make
changes in your eating habits. You may like
to take a vitamin and mineral supplement,
as the body uses more B-vitamins, vitamin
C, and zinc when under stress. Read the

*Above: looking good can make you feel
better and increase your self-confidence.*

chapters on exercise and relaxation again
and make sure you incorporate both into
your everyday life.

LEARNING TO MANAGE YOUR TIME

This is an important part of stress-proofing your life. Try keeping a diary for a week and writing down in detail how you spend your time. Be specific and break it down as much as possible. For example, 10 minutes going to the shop to buy a newspaper; 20 minutes making a cup of tea and reading a newspaper; five minutes washing and drying up the mug and plate, and so on. You'll probably be amazed at how much time you spent on unproductive or unenjoyable tasks.

Use what you have discovered to consider how well you are using your time and whether you are making the best use of your time and energy. Think about how much of your week you spend doing activities you choose compared with how much you spend reacting to other people and events. How much time did you really enjoy? The less time you are spending on the things you really want to do, the more stressed you are likely to feel.

Once you know where all your time goes, you can start to create more time. The way to do this is what the experts call "prioritizing," which simply means putting first things first.

The things we have to do can be divided into those we know are going to happen and those that crop up. The things you know are going to happen are the ones over which you have the most control. The things that crop up have to be dealt with— as quickly as possible to get them out of

the way if you can, so plan in some free time slots for them. Here are some suggestions for how you can do this.

■ List the jobs and activities you have to do that have a deadline or have to be completed by a certain date. These are your urgent jobs.

■ Next list the jobs and activities you have to do that could have serious consequences if left undone, such as going to have a cervical smear or visiting the dentist. These are your important jobs.

■ Finally list the jobs and activities that if not done urgently could have serious consequences. For instance, if you don't pay your phone bill within the next seven days you risk your telephone being cut off. These are your important and urgent jobs.

■ From now on, aim to avoid letting things fall into list three by planning ahead. For example, if you have a tendency to forget to pay your phone bill, don't wait until you get the final demand informing you that you are about to be cut off. Make a date in your diary of when you have to pay it by, or, alternatively, set up a system of payment through your bank so that your bill is paid automatically.

Opposite: managing your time effectively is a very important part of stress management. Be sure to make time for yourself as well as for work, and build in some relaxing activities which will help reduce stress.

■ Now look at jobs in list one. Some items on this list may be able to be shelved altogether. Which ones can wait; which ones will go away if you don't do them? And which ones do you have to get done? Write these into your diary, making sure you leave enough time to complete them.

■ This leaves jobs or activities in list two: the important things. These are things you know are going to happen and by and large choose to make happen which are also important to you.

■ It is vital to allow yourself enough time to do what you plan to do. Otherwise you risk having to rush or botching a job, which is likely to be counter-productive and stressful. Things usually take twice as long as you imagine—allowing for things going wrong, trains breaking down, unexpected problems and so on—so when setting yourself a time goal, try to be realistic. Write down an estimate of how long you think it will take, and then double it.

SOME QUESTIONS TO ASK YOURSELF

When faced with a task ask yourself the following questions:

■ "Is it really necessary?"

■ "Is it the best way to use my time?"

■ "Do I really want to use my time this way?"

If the answers are "No," then don't do them, or otherwise schedule them in for non-peak times.

SIMPLE WAYS TO CREATE MORE TIME

■ Get up an hour earlier.

■ Go to bed an hour later.

■ Put something less important off.

■ Learn to do routine tasks faster.

■ Use time spent traveling or waiting for trains, buses, at the dentist or doctor's surgery for reading, dreaming, or writing. Don't spend it raging over the delay!

BALANCING YOUR TIME

The least stressed people are those who achieve a balance between all the different strands in their life. Inevitably there will be occasions when you choose to spend more time or energy on one particular area. For instance, if you are on vacation with your partner you can forget about time spent with friends, except perhaps for sending them a postcard, and concentrate on enjoying yourself and the time you spend together.

Accept that there will be times when time gets out of balance, for example, if you are moving house, going to college or returning to learning, having a baby, a new relationship, or change in an existing relationship. The least stressful way to cope is to prepare yourself and others who are likely to be affected that they are about to happen and will demand more of your time and energy than usual.

PUTTING IT ALL TOGETHER

STRESS MANAGEMENT PLAN
Cathy

Cathy, 18, is leaving home to go to college. It's the first time she has lived away from home and she is worried about finding somewhere to live, managing on a tight budget, organizing her work load, and making new friends. Katy's plan might be something along the following lines.

■ **Source of stress**
Finding somewhere to live.
■ **Action**
Contact the accommodation officer at college for a list of student properties; go down a month or so before and buy local newspapers.

■ **Source of stress**
Managing on a grant.
■ **Action**
Contact bank manager to discuss opening a student account; read a book on budgeting; work out budget.

■ **Source of stress**
Organizing workload.
■ **Action**
Get timetable from college to see lectures, tutorials and seminars. Draw up a time management plan.

■ **Source of stress**
Making friends.
■ **Action**
Find out what clubs and organizations there are at the college; find out if anyone from school is going to the same college; make a point of being friendly as most new students will have the same feelings of anxiety.

STRESS MANAGEMENT PLAN

Rachel

Rachel, 32, is expecting her first baby. She is worried about the birth, how she will juggle looking after a baby and work, and how having a baby will affect her relationship with her partner. Rachel's stress management plan might involve the following.

- **Source of stress**

Giving birth.

- **Action**

Read books and magazines on birth; talk to midwife; talk to friends who have had babies; find out about birth preparation classes.

- **Source of stress**

Worry about how having a baby will affect relationship with partner.

- **Action**

Share worries with partner; make a plan for sharing childcare; organize regular evening out.

- **Source of stress**

Juggling looking after a baby and work.

- **Action**

Decide how long to take off work and inform employer; find out about rights and responsibilities; think about different forms of childcare—ask friends who have had babies/read books; advertise for someone to look after the baby/go to look at nurseries and local childcare facilities.

STRESS MANAGEMENT PLAN

Ruth

Ruth is 45. Her last child is about to leave home and she is thinking of going back to work but does not know what career to pursue. She feels that she and her husband have grown away from each other in recent years and is worried about her relationship.

■ **Source of stress**
Going back to work.

■ **Action**
Find out what job opportunities are available in area; consider career counseling; find out whether further training is needed; find out if there are any courses locally.

■ **Source of stress**
Relationship with husband.

■ **Action**
Make more quality time to talk to each other; arrange a vacation; if communication has really broken down, seek professional counseling.

STRESS MANAGEMENT IN A NUTSHELL

■ **Be prepared** Worrying won't conquer stress. Having a plan of action will. Do it today rather than waiting for situations to build up and get worse.

■ **Banish negatives** Think positively and believe you can deal with problems.

■ **Look after yourself** Watch your diet, cut down on alcohol, convenience foods, and artificial stimulants, and make sure you plan for exercise and relaxation.

■ **Learn to manage your time effectively** Planning in advance will help create time to do what you want.

■ **Learn to laugh** Try not to take life too seriously. Learn to see the funny side of things.

■ **Try a little tenderness** Pamper yourself. Take some time out every day to do something you enjoy doing.

■ **Keep tabs on your stress** Every week assess your stress levels and work out action plans for dealing with stress. Keep an eye on your progress.

■ **Express your feelings** Don't bottle up your feelings. Learn to express them.

■ **Seek help** Know the warning signs and if you are finding it all too overwhelming don't be afraid to seek professional help.

USEFUL ADDRESSES

UNITED STATES

AROMATHERAPY
National Association for Holistic
Aromatherapy
P.O. Box 17622
Boulder
CO 80308

ACUPUNCTURE
American Medical Acupuncture
Association
7535 Laurel Canyon Boulevard, Suite C
North Hollywood
CA 91605

ALEXANDER TECHNIQUE
North American Society of Teachers of
the Alexander Technique
PO Box 517
Urbana
IL 61801
Tel: (800) 473–0620

AROMATHERAPY
National Association for Holistic
Aromatherapy
219 Carl Street
San Francisco
CA 94117–3804
Tel: (415) 564–6785

FLOWER ESSENCES
Flower Essence Society
PO Box 459
Nevada City
CA 95959
Tel: (800) 548–0075

HERBAL THERAPY
The American Herbalists Guild
PO Box 1683
Soquel
CA 95073
Tel: (408) 464–2441

HOMEOPATHY
International Foundation for
Homeopathy
2366 Eastlake Avenue
Suite 325
Seattle
WA 98102
Tel: (206) 324–8230

HYPNOTHERAPY
American Board of
Hypnotherapy
16842 Von Karman Avenue
Suite 475
Irvine
CA 92714–4950
Tel: (714) 261–6400

MASSAGE

American Massage Therapy Association
820 Davis Street, Suite 100
Evanston
IL 60201–4444
Tel: (708) 864–0123

NATUROPATHY

American Association of Naturopathic Physicians
2366 Eastlake Avenue
E Suite 322
Seattle
WA 98102
Tel: (206) 323–7610

OSTEOPATHY

American Osteopathic Association
142 E Ontario Street
Chicago
IL 60611

POLARITY THERAPY

American Polarity Therapy Association
2888 Bluff Street
Suite 149
Boulder
CO 80301
Tel: (303) 545–2080

REFLEXOLOGY

International Institute of Reflexology
PO Box 12642
St. Petersburg

FL 33733–2642
Tel: (813) 343–4811

ROLFING

The Rolf Institute of Structural Integration
205 Canyon Boulevard
Boulder
CO 80302
Tel: (800) 530 8875

UNITED KINGDOM

For information on courses in most forms of Complementary Medicine, you should contact:
The Institute for Complementary Medicine
Unit 15
Tavern Quay
Commercial Centre
Rope Street
London SE16 1TX
Tel: 0171 237 5165

For information on registered practitioners in most forms of Complementary Medicine, you should contact:
The British Register of Complementary Practitioners
P.O. Box 194
London SE16 1QZ

BRCP Divisions include:
Aromatherapy, Chromotherapy, Colour, Chinese Medicine, Energy Medicine, Counselling, Healing Counselling, Herbal Medicine, Homeopathy, Medical

Hypnotherapy, Psychotherapy, Indian Medicine, Japanese Medicine, Physical Medicine (Alexander Technique, Osteopathy, Chiropractic, Remedial Massage, Massage, Nutritional Medicine, Reflexology and others), Diagnostic systems: Iridology, Kinesiology, Signalysis. Professional techniques include: Heller Work, Rolfing, Bach Flower Remedies, Bates Eye Care.

International Stress and Management Association
25 Sutherland Road
Roundhay
Leeds LS8 1BY

Relaxation for Living
29 Burwood Park Road
Walton on Thames
Surrey KT12 5HL

British Association for Counselling
1 Regent Place
Rugby
Warwickshire
CO21 2PJ

MIND (National Association for Mental Health)
22 Harley Street
London W1

Defeat Depression Campaign
The Royal College of Psychiatrists
17 Belgrave Square
London SW1X 8PG

Samaritans National Helpline
Tel: 0345 909090
(you can call even if you are not feeling suicidal)

AROMATHERAPY

International Federation of Aromatherapists
Stamford House
2–4 Chiswick High Road
London W4 1TH

International Society of Professional Aromatherapists
ISPA House
82 Ashby Road
Hinckley
Leicestershire.
LE10 1SF

AUSTRALIA

Association of Massage Therapists
19a Spit Road
Mosman
NSW 2088

Association of Remedial Masseurs
22 Stuart Street
Ryde NSW 2112

International Federation of Aromatherapists
(Australian branch) Inc.
5 Uren Place
Kambahact 2902
Australia
Tel/fax: Australia 06 231 0707

FURTHER READING

STRESS, ANXIETY AND DEPRESSION

Gillett, Dr. Richard, *Overcoming Depression* (Dorling Kindersley)
Hartley, Mary, *The Good Stress Guide* (Sheldon Press)
Holmes, Ros and Jeremy, *The Good Mood Guide* (Orion)
Kenton, Leslie, *Beat Stress* (Vermilion)
Kirsta, Alix, *The Book of Stress Survival* (Unwin Paperbacks)
Lewis, Dr. Davis, *10 Minute Time and Stress Management* (Piatkus)
Needham, Alix, *The Stress Management Book* (Virgin)
Roet, Dr. Brian, *A Safer Place to Cry* (Optima)
Westcott, Patsy, *How to Get What You Want* (Bloomsbury)
Westcott, Patsy, *The Survivor Personality* (Bloomsbury)

COMPLEMENTARY MEDICINE, YOGA AND MEDITATION

Brown, Denis, *Massage* (Headway)
Ferguson, Pamela, *The Self-Shiatsu Handbook* (Boxtree)
Jarmey, Chris, and Tindall, John, *Acupressure for Common Ailments* (Gaia)
Harrold, Fiona, *The Massage Manual*
(Headline)
Kenton, Leslie, *Ultrahealth* (Arrow)
Maxwell-Hudson, Clare, *The Complete Book of Massage* (Dorling Kindersley)
Murray, Michael T., *Stress, Anxiety and Insomnia* (Prima Publishing)
Nagarathna, Dr. R., Nagendra, Dr. H.R., and Monro, Dr. Robin, *Yoga for Common Ailments* (Gaia)
Vaughan, Sue, *Finding the Stillness Within in a Busy World* (C.W. Daniel Company Ltd)
Young, Jacqueline, *Self-Massage* (Thorsons)

AROMATHERAPY

Bradford, Nicky, *The Well Woman's Self Help Directory*
Bradford, Nicky, *Men's Health Matters*
Bradford, Nicky, *Hamlyn's Encyclopedia of Complementary Medicine*
Davis, P., *The A to Z of Aromatherapy*
Grayson, Jane, *The Fragrant Year*
Lawrence, Brian, *Essential Oils*
Lunny, Dr. V., *I.F.A. Times Articles*
M. Maury, *The secret of life and youth*
Price, S., *Practical Aromatherapy*
Tisserand, R., *Aromatherapy for Everyone*
Valnet, Dr. J., *Aromatherapie*
Werner, Monica, *Aromatherapie*
Werner, Monica, *Sanfte Massage*
Worwood, V.A., *The Fragrant Pharmacy*

INDEX